Psychology and the Natural Law of Reparation

C. FRED ALFORD

University of Maryland

CAMBRIDGE
UNIVERSITY PRESS

CAMBRIDGE UNIVERSITY PRESS
Cambridge, New York, Melbourne, Madrid, Cape Town, Singapore, São Paulo

Cambridge University Press
40 West 20th Street, New York, NY 10011-4211, USA

www.cambridge.org
Information on this title: www.cambridge.org/9780521863322

First published 2006

Printed in the United States of America

A catalog record for this publication is available from the British Library.

Library of Congress Cataloging in Publication Data
Alford, C. Fred.
Psychology and the natural law of reparation / C. Fred Alford.
p.   cm.
Includes bibliographical references and index.
ISBN 0-521-86332-5 (hardback)
1. Reparation (Psychoanalysis).   2. Natural law.   3. Psychology.
4. Psychotherapy.   I. Title.
RC489.R48A44   2006
616.89′14–dc22   2005031158

ISBN-13   978-0-521-86332-2 hardback
ISBN-10   0-521-86332-5 hardback

Contents

v

Preface

The idea that Melanie Klein might be a natural law theorist has been marinating with me for some time. That she might actually fulfill the requirements of traditional natural law thinking only came to me after reading and teaching the great Thomist of the twentieth century, Jacques Maritain. I cannot say for certain why, only that while Maritain is a deeply religious man, he locates natural law in a space different from where Aquinas locates the natural law. For Aquinas, natural law remains an aspect of Eternal Law. For Maritain (and some readers will think that I have already tipped my hand), natural law owes almost as much to the phenomenology of his early teacher, Henri Bergson, as it does to Catholic theology. This is so, even if this is not an aspect of the natural law that Maritain talked or wrote about in later years.

Nevertheless, neither Maritain nor any other natural law theorist has paid sufficient attention to natural evil. This is something I always wonder about when I go to conferences where people try hard to convince one another that the natural law exists. Or if it doesn't, then universals such as those written about by Kant or Rawls must. Or if not that, then at least the moral sentiments must exist, such as those written about by Adam Smith and David Hume. But if that's true, then why do people generally behave so badly? Why was the twentieth century the bloodiest in world history, more than one hundred million killed in warfare, more than one hundred sixty million if one includes genocide and "democide," as it is called, such as the mass murders of Stalin and Mao? Perhaps it makes more sense to begin with the sources of natural

vii

evil, if I may call them that, and then go on to look for the sources and forces that may counteract the human pleasure in destruction. For that is what we are talking about when we talk about evil, at least in the roughly secular context that I am going to talk about good and evil.

Here is where Melanie Klein makes her great contribution, beginning with evil, assuming that we have hated before we have loved, that we have wished to destroy before we have wished to create. Of all the great figures in the history of the natural law, only Saint Augustine came close to her insight, and then only for a moment. For Klein, natural law grows out of a desire to make reparation for the world of hatred and destruction that lies within. That dimension of natural law has never been adequately addressed by those who would find the good in each of us, and the world we share together, the good that is the basis of the natural law.

Though my book is organized around this thesis, the path is winding. Chapter 2 is based on interviews with a number of young informants, as I call them, asking them how they would respond to someone who seemed to reject outright the most basic assumptions of the natural law, particularly as expressed in the United Nations Declaration of Human Rights.

Other chapters consider the new natural law theorists, as they are called, such as John Finnis and Robert George, as well as the evolutionary natural law, as it is called. I take particular pains to show that Klein, and those who follow her, such as Wilfred Bion and D. W. Winnicott, truly work within the tradition established by Augustine, Aquinas, and particularly Maritain. Finally, I argue that while Hannah Arendt's study of the evil of men such as Adolf Eichmann would seem to be helpful in drawing the connection between Augustine and Klein, in the end Arendt fails to grasp evil. This is doubly disappointing, as Arendt's dissertation was devoted to Augustine, and she seems to have drawn her well-known concept of the "banality of evil" from Augustine's concept of evil as the privation of the good. That, it turns out, is precisely the problem. Evil is far more than the privation of the good: it is the willful destruction of the good because it is good, and not me or mine. Milton's Satan in *Paradise Lost* is one of the few literary characters to know that dimension of evil. Only when we do, I argue, can we truly appreciate the natural law of reparation.

Two anonymous reviewers for Cambridge University Press were enormously helpful in seeing the value of my project, while pointing out where my argument fell short. I have not always met their objections, but their comments were never far from my mind.

My colleague, Jim Glass, read a next-to-last draft, pointing out where I was less than clear, while understanding my main point with special clarity. Once again I owe him more than words can express. Since I shared this project with him so late in the game, he is particularly blameless for my errors and omissions.

My wife, Elly, and my family have provided me endless opportunities to make reparation. Sometimes I think that this is what families are for.

Antigone and the Natural Law

My approach to the natural law is inspired by an article by Henry Veatch, "Natural Law: Dead or Alive?" originally published in 1978.[1] After a brief but encyclopedic review of the natural law since Saint Thomas Aquinas, whom he interprets in good Aristotelian fashion, Veatch concludes that even today those who talk about rights remain dependent on a natural law they do not acknowledge. Consider Alan Gewirth's *Reason and Morality* (1978), which argues that human agents must recognize that their actions are both purposive, as well as voluntary and free. Furthermore, to recognize this is to recognize that this state of affairs is good. But, to acknowledge that this is true for me is also to acknowledge that it must be good for any and every other human being.

Veatch (2005) asks why is this the only rational response? Why could someone not respond roughly as follows? Sure, I'm glad that I am in a position to act freely and purposefully as a human being. But, I don't claim freedom and purpose as a right, since it is nothing more than a simple fact about my individual situation, albeit a very happy fact. Thus, there is no way in which I am logically bound to recognize a corresponding right to freedom and purpose on the part of other

---

[1] Henry Veatch, "Natural Law: Dead or Alive?" The essay is now most readily found at The Online Library of Liberty, Liberty Fund, <http://oll.libertyfund.org/Texts/LiteratureOfLiberty0352/BibliographicEssays/VeatchNaturalLaw.html>. Cited as Veatch 2005.

human beings. In other words, Kantian universalism does not avoid the appeal to natural law, no matter what clothes it wears, and that includes the celebrated attire of John Rawls (1999).

We are, it seems, at the end of the road. Universalistic approaches from Kant to Rawls and beyond cannot fulfill their own claims to self-justification. But the natural law seems to depend on an obsolete metaphysics, in which everything in nature is headed toward its proper goal. Kai Nielsen (1988) puts it this way.

The natural moral law theory only makes sense in terms of an acceptance of medieval physics and cosmology. If we give up the view that the universe is purposive and that all motions are just so many attempts to reach the changeless, we must give up natural moral law theories. One might say, as a criticism of the Thomistic doctrine of natural moral law, that since medieval physics is false then it follows that natural moral law theory must be false. (1988, 212)

Let us not despair, responds Veatch. Recent developments in the philosophy of science, developments inspired by Karl Popper (2002), and elaborated by Thomas Kuhn (1996) and Paul Feyerabend (1993), have revealed that science is not the one true picture of the world, but one of many pictures.

For if science is not concerned with nature as it really is in itself, then modern science cannot be said to have undermined that conception of nature in terms of which all operations in nature, and particularly those operations characteristic of human beings, might be said to have there fore-conceived natural ends. In other words, there could be no basic incompatibility between what the scientists have to say about nature and the concept of nature that is required by a natural law or natural rights philosophy. (Veatch 2005)

Though Veatch is my inspiration, his is not my argument. What counts for humans is not nature but narratives. Veatch liberates us from the false dilemma that either our narratives must be scientific (which today often takes the form of evolutionary biology as natural law, discussed in Chapter 4), or they are "just narratives." Well, it's all just narrative. Some narratives are just better than others: deeper, more awesome, more manifold, more fulfilling, more in touch with human nature. Of course, mine is just an assertion. To back it up, I would have to tell a particular story, setting it against other stories, in order to show why the story I tell is better. That is what I intend to do in this book.

Once one begins to tell a story, however, a troubling insight quickly occurs. Since Aristotle's day, more than one plausible narrative of the good human life has emerged:

The life of the aesthete, who makes of his existence a work of art. Oscar Wilde is exemplary.

Nietzsche's modern day version of the Greek warrior, the *Übermensch*.

The absurd hero, represented Dr. Rieux in *The Plague*, by Albert Camus (1972). In the midst of horror and loss, the admirable doctor fights "against creation as he found it" (120). Trouble is, Meursault of Camus's *The Stranger*, while possibly pathetic, is arguably as admirable as Rieux, living and dying without compromise, resisting society as he found it.

This list is just a beginning. My approach is to argue for a particular vision of the good life for men and women, one that takes seriously a comment by Leo Strauss (1999, 180), but in a sense never intended by him when he characterizes Machiavelli's and Hobbes's visions of natural law as ones in which "the complete basis of natural law must be sought, not in the end of man, but in his beginnings."

The beginnings Strauss refers to include fear, greed, hate, lust, and the like. I turn to the psychoanalyst Melanie Klein in order to characterize this beginning, arguing that besides fear, greed, hate, and lust, are primitive but hardly simple desires to love, care for, and make reparation to those we have hated and harmed in phantasy or reality. The task of natural law is to work with these desires in order to make them moral.

It turns out that the content of a roughly Kleinian vision of natural law, the natural law of reparation, comes close to the content of natural law as it is conceived by Thomas Aquinas, and particularly Jacques Maritain. A thoroughly secular woman, Klein was nonetheless an essentially religious thinker, by which I mean that her basic categories of thought were the categories of original sin, trespass, guilt, and salvation through reparation.

It is within this framework that I will be arguing, and ultimately it is at this level that arguments about the natural law must be carried out today if they are to be worthwhile. When I say "at this level," I do not mean, of course, that arguments about natural law today must invoke Klein or psychoanalysis. I mean that arguments about the natural law should tell a particular story about the good life for men and women. Continuing to argue whether natural law is possible is an enterprise of diminishing returns. While it remains necessary to introduce and contextualize the discussion of natural law in terms of difficult issues of epistemology and methodology, the more pressing task today is to go out and do the natural law in order to see how convincing we can be, both to ourselves and to others.

At one level, my argument about the natural law will sound familiar. What Melanie Klein calls reparation, the desire to make amends for the harm we have done, or wished to do, to others, can be interpreted in terms of *caritas*. Unlike Eros, caritas cares more for the other than one's own satisfaction. Indeed, I will argue that the caritas of reparation stems from a love for the goodness of the world that is akin to the goodness that both Saint Augustine and Aquinas see as the foundation of the natural law. In one respect, but in one respect only, the origin of the natural law in what Klein calls reparation is straightforward.

Two barriers stand in the way of realizing the natural law of reparation. Indeed, if I could not explain to you why the power of the natural law remains largely latent, then you must think me a fool. For everywhere one looks one sees not goodness and caritas, but hate, suspicion, and destruction, at least at the level of society, and unfortunately in many families as well.

The first barrier is that one cannot get to reparation without passing through the dominion of death. In this chapter, Antigone will represent the kingdom of death, particularly its confusion with life. This confusion I will call dark Eros, the confusion of Eros with the *Todestrieb*, as Freud called the death drive, the love of annihilation. The need to make reparation is so strong because we have longed to destroy the innocent, the pure, and the good. Not just in order to possess these attributes for ourselves, but because there is a deep and perverse pleasure in the destruction of goodness itself. Reparation, indeed caritas, stem from the horror that humans feel when they come to know (even if this knowledge remains no more than intuition) the power of these destructive forces in themselves.

To know natural law we must know natural evil, which I shall define as the insistent presence of the death drive within and behind so much of what humans do. The traditional natural law has never addressed the problem of evil with the seriousness it deserves, even as Augustine came close for a moment. But perhaps putting it this way is too unhistorical, even for a work on the natural law. Perhaps it has taken the twentieth century, the bloodiest in world history, to confront us with the *Todestrieb* in all its bloody glory. In any case, I will argue that even as it has failed to give evil its due, only the traditional natural law – the natural law of Augustine, Thomas Aquinas, and Jacques Maritain – comes close to that of the natural law of reparation. Close, but not close enough.

Here, I believe, is what makes my account of natural law distinctive. Not just that I draw upon a psychoanalyst to make my point, while taking seriously the claims of the traditional natural law throughout, above all that it join nature and moral obligation. The natural law is not just another term for universalism, whatever the species: Kantian, anthropological, or evolutionary. My commitment to the traditional natural law is important, but it is not the key to my account, except in the following sense. Klein must meet the standards of the traditional natural law in order to be considered a natural law theorist. She receives no special dispensation.

Singular is my argument that natural law must take into account the pleasure in destruction – not just dark Eros, but the human desire to destroy the good because it is good, and not me or mine. Milton's Satan (*Paradise Lost* IV, 40–55, 105–110) comes closest to representing this vision of evil, for that is what it is, and I believe that the natural law of reparation is the only vision of natural law that comes to terms with this reality, which is unfortunately not confined to Satan, but is shared to some degree by us all.

Those familiar with the psychoanalytic theory of Melanie Klein will, I believe, readily understand how one could interpret the natural law in terms of her category of reparation, which she already understands in quasi-religious terms as an act of contrition through which we work for absolution from our thoughts and deeds of greed, hatred, and destruction. What I add is that reparation as an account of the natural law only makes sense once one accepts that we are first of all creatures who have wanted to destroy all that is good and life-giving. We have hated before we have loved. In the end, our love may be stronger than our hate, but hate comes first. Some may think they recognize the story of the Fall and Salvation. I would prefer to say that Biblical themes do not a religion make. Postmoderns or not, believers or not, in the West we all still live in the penumbra of the Judeo-Christian tradition, and that is all that is necessary to accept my account.

And yet Kleinian reparation is entirely inadequate as an account of the natural law. This is the second barrier to a strictly Kleinian account. Reparation is morally untrustworthy, as likely to be satisfied by painting a picture about the terrible deeds one has done as by making amends to the actual victims. Reparation tends, in other words, to get stuck within the cave of one's mind. How to draw reparation out of one's imagination into the world? How to direct reparation toward those one has harmed, and their real-world stand-ins, the needy, the desperate, and the despised? In order to answer this question I first elaborate on the Kleinian account using the work of Wilfred Bion and D. W. Winnicott, both independent-minded students of hers.

Next, I turn to the natural law, particularly as it is interpreted by Jacques Maritain. Natural law not only provides the moral guidance that reparation requires, but the natural law of Maritain has affinities to the work of Klein. In order to make this argument, I must introduce a third party, and a third term. The third party is Winnicott, who is a remarkably subtle theorist of community, a communitarian for whom the individual remains paramount. The third term is "personalism," a doctrine explicitly held by Maritain, and implicitly (unacknowledged and likely unrecognized) by Winnicott. In order to give all these abstractions some substance, I argue that the "dignitarian" tradition (Glendon 2001, 42, 227) of human rights reflected in the preamble to the United Nations Declaration of Human Rights reflects the perspective of personalism.

Personalism is not only a theological-political doctrine. Personalism reflects the social and political conditions under which reparative thinking is possible, conditions that I will call, following Winnicott, containment. Containment begins with family, and comes to include all of a decent society, from the stories it tells about itself, to its police and welfare programs, to its retirement security. Containment is a combination of loving personal relationships and a decent social compact. Cultural containment is provision of the support necessary for reparation and thought to talk with each other, and with the world. Absent containment, thinking is too terrifying, and reparation too self-indulgent. It is the combination of reparation and thought that together constitutes the natural law. In other words, the realization of the natural law depends upon some fairly straightforward, but nonetheless exceptional, social conditions. Much of Chapter 4 is concerned with this topic.

I am summarizing my argument, not my book, which follows a slightly different order. The remainder of this chapter is concerned with how close death comes to life in Antigone's appeal to the natural law. I say this not to deny Antigone's historical claim to embody the natural law, but to demonstrate the dark powers anyone who takes the natural law seriously must confront. Greek tragedy is significant for another reason as well. Greek tragedy does not just illustrate containment; it embodies it. The very act of watching a tragedy at Athens was an instance of containment, framing and forming otherwise unbearable emotions. Indeed, this is the best way to interpret Aristotle's definition of tragedy (he was referring to the experience of attending the performance) as the *katharsis* of pity and fear (*Poetics*, c. 6).

Chapter 2 devotes little attention to Klein, more attention to the traditional natural law, and a great deal of attention to a group of young people; informants I call them. Originally I had planned to read several articles from the UN Declaration to them, asking informants if they agreed, why, and what they would say to someone who disagreed. As it turns out, I asked several additional questions, but reading of a couple of articles from the UN Declaration, accompanied by a question along the lines of "What would you say to someone who said that Article 1 [or 3] is the stupidest thing I ever heard?" remained the leitmotiv of my research for Chapter 2.

Informants, I argue, are hardly personalists. But neither are they the liberals, relativists, cynics (in the contemporary sense), or subjective individualists that Alasdair MacInyre, Alan Bloom, and other culture critics claim to find among the young. On the contrary, most informants hold to a minimal version of the natural law. How much of a teaching opportunity this minimal commitment to the natural law provides cultural workers should not be underestimated. Beyond question, this commitment provides a remarkable learning opportunity for all cultural workers, especially university professors and other so-called experts in the intellectual Zeitgeist.

ANTIGONE

What kind of life would lead people not just to be ignorant of the natural law, but to find the very concept incomprehensible? Alasdair

MacIntyre's (2000) answer is the culture of advanced modernity – that is, the culture in which almost all of us live everyday. In this culture the individual is the alpha and the omega, the beginning and the end of every question, and every answer. Contrast this culture with that of Thomas Aquinas, in which people understood themselves as members of a larger human community, one in which the human good is naturally shared. Only in such a community does the natural law naturally make sense.

George Steiner asks a similar question about Sophocles' Antigone, a traditional heroine of the natural law. If the "gods' unwritten and unfailing laws" are of manifest universality and eternity, why are they not clear to Creon, or to the chorus of Theban elders?[2] Indeed, one might argue that they are apparent to no one but Antigone. Though Haimon, Antigone's fiancé (and Creon's son), objects to the punishment his father would inflict, burying Antigone alive, Haimon's motives appear to have little to do with the natural law. Love for Antigone, resentment at his father, a concern for public opinion: these are what seem to motivate Haimon. Or perhaps these motives do concern the natural law, but the connection is tortuous. We shall see.

If natural law is so natural, why is Antigone the only one who seems to get it? Because she is outside the categories of both polis and history, human constructions that remove us from a direct encounter with the natural law, which resides somewhere less temporal and historical than community. About this encounter, I would add, it is one that humans cannot long abide in solitude and continue to live. Steiner puts it this way.

The answer is that for Antigone the polis and the category of the historical – of rationally organized and mastered timeliness – have obtruded, irrelevantly and then destructively, upon an order of being, call it 'familial,' 'telluric,' 'cyclical,' in which man was, literally, at home in timelessness. Such at-homeness before or outside history makes of philia, of 'loving immediacy,' of 'unquestioning care,' the rule of human relations. It is in this very definite sense that the unwritten laws of loving care which Antigone cites, and which she places under

---

[2] *Antigone*, line 456. The translation I use is that of Elizabeth Wyckoff, in the Chicago University Press series, edited by David Grene and Richmond Lattimore (1954). Occasionally, when the Greek seems especially important, I turn to the Loeb Classical Library edition of *Antigone*, published by Harvard University Press, which has the Greek on one page, an English translation by F. Storr on the opposite page.

the twofold aegis of Olympian Zeus and chthonian dike, are 'natural law.' They embody an imperative of humaneness which men and women share before they enter into the mutations, the transitory illusion, the divisive experiments of a historical and political system. Creon does not and cannot answer. For time does not answer, or indeed, bandy words with eternity. (Steiner 1986, 250–251)

How different Steiner's answer is from MacIntyre's. For MacIntyre, as for most of the traditional natural law theorists, such as Aquinas, we know the natural law by living in community with others.[3] For Steiner, we know the natural law most clearly when we live as outcast, unable to participate fully in all those aspects of community life that bind us in a fleshy human web of dialogue with others, the mundane chat of everyday life that distracts from first principles. Antigone is in communion with eternity, to which she already belongs, partly by choice, primarily by chance of incestuous birth, which excludes her from normal community.

How can we count thee Antigone? Why have you cast such a spell on the Western imagination, so that between circa 1790 and 1905, many European poets, philosophers, and scholars held that Sophocles' *Antigone* was not only the finest Greek tragedy, but a work of art nearer to perfection than any other ever produced (Steiner 1986, 1)? Indeed, Antigone has been seen under numerous horizons: As a prefiguration of Christ, including virginity, nocturnal burial, sacrificial love, action as compassion, and finally heroism as freely shared agony.

As a Jungian archetype, whose details we need not go into, except to say that this archetype is almost as readily rendered in terms of the structural anthropology of Levi-Strauss, in which our fundamental myths correspond to certain primordial social confrontations, such as between man and woman, young and old, and above all between life and death, being and nonbeing. Indeed, Steiner speculates that the "mytho-logic" at issue in Antigone may lie so deep as to reflect "the axial, the symmetrical, structure of the brain and of the body," which

---

[3] It's not simple. For Aquinas, we first learn the natural law through an individual encounter with the goodness of God's creation (ST I–I 79, 12). Communal dialogue frames this experience; it does not create it.

come to represent being and non-being itself, life and death (Steiner 1986, 128).

Because I will be drawing upon the work of the psychoanalyst Melanie Klein, one might be inclined to read Klein's almost legendary distinction between the good breast and the bad breast along these lines, as a type of natural law built into the symmetrical structure of mothers' bodies. This is not my argument. Not breasts or bodies, but narratives are the primordial structures I am most interested in.

Not just a primordial narrative, Antigone is also a conversation in at least two senses. First, *Antigone*, like all Greek tragedy, was originally presented as part of a conversation within the Athenian polis. Antigone may have been *apolis* (απολις), one without a city or country, but the play in which she is the protagonist was presented in the theater of Dionysus as part of a civic festival, the Great (or City) Dionysia. Antigone is the antagonist, one who is born to stand against and alone, but her story is presented as part of a civic ceremony of collective self-assertion.[4]

The tension between tragedy, which is generally (and certainly in the case of *Antigone*) an assertion of the primacy of family, and a love that has little to do with the polis, and the framework within which this assertion took place, the polis celebrating itself, has struck many observers. In other words, the polis provided a framework within which forces that are irrelevant if not hostile to politics, such as erotic and even familial love, could be addressed in all their anarchic complexity.

In fact, it's not so simple, as Judith Butler (2000) argues in *Antigone's Claim: Kinship between Life and Death*. Though Hegel, as well as Steiner, would set the family against the polis, the family has always had the job of preparing its members for life in the polis: as soldiers, producers in the household economy, and so forth. While "the personal is the

---

[4] Performed once or twice a year, it seems wrong to call the tragedies plays. If, that is, the term "play" suggests a night out at the theater. In classical Athens, the price of a theater ticket was distributed by the local *deme* or district to citizens in good standing. Citizens sat in the open-air theater below the Acropolis in wedge-shaped sections designated for each of the ten demes, just as they did for a meeting of the assembly. The audience was overwhelmingly, perhaps exclusively male, and was likely composed of the same few thousand citizens who attended the forty annual meetings of the assembly. In other words, the theater was an extension of the democratic assembly, an impression strengthened by the fact that the chorus was composed (in all likelihood) of *ephebes*, young men in the first two years of their military service (Winkler and Zeitlin 1990).

political" is a contemporary slogan, its truth goes back a couple of thousand years. We should think twice about setting family against polis, as though this were a fundamental, "telluric" opposition, for it is not.

What we need to look for is aspects of family life that are so primitive that they are destructive not just of political life, but of life itself. This is what the tragic playwrights grasped, the threat posed by regressive, destructive forces within the family, Not just Sophocles' *Antigone*, but Aeschylus' *Oresteia*, Melanie Klein's favorite tragedy, is about this threat, as are most other tragedies.[5] Indeed, this is what Aristotle means when he writes of tragedy as having happened virtually by accident upon that one theme that would bring pity and fear to us all just by its very telling – dramas in which family members are destroyed by those they love (*Poetics*, c. 14).

Steiner's book is titled *Antigones*, and it concerns the hundreds of Antigones who have entered Western literature and art. Perhaps the most famous, at least as far as it aims to transform an essentially ineffable encounter with eternity into dialogue (dialectic) is Hegel's (1920) use of Sophocles' *Antigone* as his archetype of the dialectic. The claims of eternal law represented by Antigone are met by the equally valid but incompatible claims of the state to its own survival, a claim represented by her Uncle Creon. It is on this basis that Hegel famously defines tragedy as the confrontation between two abstract rights, both of which cannot prevail.

It matters little whether Hegel misunderstands, and hence trivializes, Antigone's claim by putting it on a level commensurate with Creon's. In fact, it may even be misleading to make Hegel's reading important, in so far as he does not merely enter into dialectic *with* the play. Instead, he transforms the play into the model of all dialectic. On the contrary, there is something fundamentally undialectical about the play. One does not bandy words with eternity, as Steiner puts it. "The whole force of the Hegelian revision of Sophocles' *Antigone* lies in Hegel's attempt to redress this unbalance and to

---

[5] Klein's "Some Reflections on 'The Oresteia'" (1975g) was incomplete but largely finished at the time of her death in 1960, and published in 1963. It is the only Greek tragedy she wrote about at length, and can be considered her version of the Oedipus myth so central to Freud. I make this argument in "Melanie Klein and the *Oresteia* Complex" (1990).

achieve that form of dialogue which is known as the dialectic. Hegel is determined to give to the necessary timeliness of politics its own rights in eternity" (Steiner 1986, 251). It is hard to imagine a more mistaken project. Or, if the reader requires an argument for such an assertion, which I have no time or inclination to give here, I will put it another way. It is hard to imagine a project more contrary to the intention of Sophocles.

What is important is that Hegel, and hundreds of others, from Jean Anouilh to Bertolt Brecht to Søren Kierkegaard to Walter Hasenclever to Jacques Derrida to the latest BBC production have tried to tell the story anew, sometimes strictly through criticism, often through a radical retelling. Rolf Hochhuth's novella, *Die Berliner Antigone* (2002), tells the story of a young woman who would substitute her body for that of her brother murdered by the Gestapo. What follows is a description of the most recent retelling I could find, one that links Antigone to the story of Argentina's disappeared. By the time you read this there will surely be another version, even more recent. The description of the play is from a press release advertising its college production. Worth commenting on is how the title connects Antigone with the furies of Aeschylus' *Oresteia*. This is a connection rarely made when writing about Sophocles' *Antigone*, and the failure to make it masks an important point, as we shall see.

'Antígona Furiosa' retells the classic story of 'Antigone,' the story of a princess wanting to bury her brother despite the law's refusal to let her do so. This retelling is placed in terms of Argentinean history, where thousands of women wanted only to know where their children were.

Known as the Mothers of the Disappeared, these women banded together to speak out against a government who had kidnapped, held, tortured and even killed these women's spouses and children. The parallel between Argentinean history and the story of Antigone helps give understanding to a classic play that may not seem relevant to today's times and also helps to show the struggles that have taken place in Argentinean life.

Griselda Gambaro, author of 'Antígona Furiosa,' wrote the play in order to challenge issues of violence, oppression, and dominance in Argentina and in today's society. Director Laura Dougherty, a graduate student at Arizona State University, finds herself deeply connected and very close to this story of Argentinean culture. She has studied the political and social situations of Latin America for years and studied in Chile for a semester during her undergraduate years. She looks at this story and this theme as a culmination of years of study, empathy, and passion and finds it a necessary message for today's audiences.

'I believe the themes of the play – struggle and remembrance, and remembrance through struggle – resound in Argentina and everywhere. It's somehow entirely hopeful despite its destitute nature,' Dougherty says.[6]

Several years earlier, the political theorist Jean Bethke Elshtain (1996) turned to Antigone to write about the same theme in a more theoretical vein in an essay titled "The Mothers of the Disappeared: An Encounter with Antigone's Daughters."

Dialectic and Incredible Stories

Why is it so important that Antigone's narrative, portrayed by Steiner as telluric, prepolitical, indeed prehistorical, not be allowed to define natural law by itself? Why is it so important that natural law be understood as the conjunction of the telluric and prepolitical with conversation – that is dialogue, the true dialectic? A dialogue that moves from stage to polis as well as across centuries, indeed millennia. Because natural law is both at once, Steiner plus MacInyre, so to speak. Natural law is a prepolitical encounter with an order that is not merely human, even as it is interpreted and known through a strictly human dialogue.

As one of its leading topics, this dialogue must recognize that the telluric forces Antigone consorts with are not just the forces of care and loving immediacy. They include the forces of self-obliteration and destruction, forces that come closer to death than to life. That's not all bad. If these forces exist, as they do, it is best to acknowledge them, but one can only do so and survive in the company of others. One way to think about these others is in terms of what Steiner calls *Antigones*, a twenty-five hundred year long conversation about the play, helping to frame and form the almost unbearable experiences Antigone evokes in all who take her seriously. In other words, history and narrative are also forms of containment.

Ironically, the natural law is more likely to be found in Steiner's *Antigones* than Sophocles' Antigone. To be sure, Steiner misreads Sophocles' play, imagining that Antigone's entrée to the natural law

---

[6] <http://herbergercollege.asu.edu/college/news/newsreleases/2002/> "Antígona Furiosa" was first produced in 2002.

stems from her access to a primordial realm prior to the polis. But this is not where Steiner goes most wrong. Where he makes his biggest mistake is in failing to grasp that this realm is not naturally pure or good or caring. On the contrary, it is a realm that comes closer to death than life. What saves Steiner, even from himself, are a couple of millennia of history – that is, two thousand plus years of conversation with and about the play, especially as this conversation takes the form of new *Antigones*. Occasionally history comes to the rescue of us all, even if it is not Hegel's history, but simply stories that never stop.

The opposite of natural law is civil law. Natural law is natural, and not merely legislative or conventional, in the same way that fire burns both here and in Persia, as Aristotle puts it (*N. Ethics* 1134b27). If we are to take the principle seriously, then we must be careful not to homogenize narrative in order to render it universal. We do not want universal to become tantamount to the lowest common denominator. We must be equally careful not to exclude from narrative those details, those particularities, and those lives that don't fit our universal story. There is, unfortunately, no guarantee that because Antigone is in touch with the telluric, the prepolitical, the timeless, the cyclical (as she is), that she automatically speaks for everyone, and for every age. There is, in other words, a particularity even to the telluric, the timeless, the prepolitical, and the cyclical. Fire burns in Persia as it burns in Greece, but every fire burns differently, depending on what it consumes, the ferocity of the wind that feeds it, and the direction from which the wind blows. Fire burns differently too depending upon whether one sees it as a case of rapid oxidation or as a tribute to the gods. Context is everything.

Only in this way do we begin to address Jean-François Lyotard (1984, xxiv), who defines the stance of postmodernism as "incredulity toward metanarratives." But what is incredulity anyway? Skepticism, the refusal to be taken in by superficial similarities – these terms apply. Incredulity toward metanarratives doesn't mean the abandonment of metanarratives. Without metanarrative we would be lost. Incredulity toward metanarratives means that we should be suspicious of metanarrative, concerned that particularity is being sacrificed. The real universality of *Antigone* resides not solely, or even primarily, in the play by that name written by Sophocles, but in the 2,500 year history of the play. It is within *this* dialectic that the natural law resides. For dialectic means dialogue: between the original narrative (and not even that was sui generis, for it drew on a dozen myths) and its retellings, which draw on a thousand personal and historical particularities expressed, forgotten, remembered, and creatively misremembered over more than two-thousand years.

DARK EROS

It would be a mistake to conclude that the natural law found in *Antigone* is only about dialogue. This is the framework that determines how we experience the content of *Antigone*, and the natural law the play expresses. But the content of the narrative remains of paramount importance.

The content most frequently referred to is Antigone as naïve natural law theorist, standing up for gods' law against humanity's. This is what she says when Creon asks her if she was aware of his proclamation against burying her brother Polyneices, and if so why she still dared break the law.

> For me it was not Zeus who made that order,
> nor did that Justice who lives with the gods below
> mark out such laws to hold among mankind.
> Nor did I think your orders were so strong
> that you, a mortal man, could over-run
> the gods' unwritten and unfailing laws.
> Not now, nor yesterday's, they always live,
> and no one knows their origin in time.
> So not through fear of any man's proud spirit
> would I be likely to neglect these laws,
> draw on myself the gods' sure punishment. (450–460)

Not so often quoted are the lines that directly follow.

> I knew that I must die; how could I not?
> even without your warning. If I die
> before my time, I say it is a gain.
> Who lives in sorrows many as are mine
> now shall he not be glad to gain his death? (461–464)

Among those who find in Antigone's words (the first words that is, the ones about the gods' unchanging laws), an ideal statement of the traditional natural law is Jacques Maritain, the great Thomist of the twentieth century. Thomas Aquinas is, in turn, *the* traditional natural law theorist; the one whom all agree is a natural law theorist, even if they agree about nothing else. Quoting from the same passage as I (but omitting lines 461–464), Maritain states that

Antigone is the heroine of natural law; she was aware of the fact that in transgressing the human law and being crushed by it, she was obeying a higher commandment – that she was obeying laws that were unwritten, and that had their origin neither today nor yesterday, but which live always and forever, and no one knows where they have come from. (Maritain 2001, 26)

In fact, the lesson about natural law is not so simple, and not just because Antigone seems over-eager to die for it. The hallmark of the play is not just the ascendancy of death over life, but the confusion of death with life, sometimes witting, sometimes not. Witting, as when Antigone talks of death as the bridegroom, the grave as her bridal chamber in which she seems so eager to spend that long night of eternity. And unwitting, Creon so confused about the basic categories of being and nonbeing that he would bury the living and fail to bury the dead.

The Eros at work in Antigone is dark Eros, the desire to care for the ones we love confused with a desire to fuse with them in death, a desire that goes together all too readily with the intentional disregard of the love of the living. "With those I love gone, I go alone and desolate," the last of my line, says Antigone (917–918). Every word she utters is false. She is evidently loved by her fiancé, Haimon, as well as her sister Ismene, who is willing to die with her even though Ismene broke no law. And Antigone is definitely not the last of her line. Ismene, who chooses life (more accurately put, is forced to choose life when her offer to die with Antigone is refused by Creon), remains.

Freud (1930, 122–123) famously writes of Eros at war with Death for the fate of the human species. True enough, but the lesson of Antigone seems a little more complicated, as none of the protagonists can keep them straight. How can Eros battle Death for the life of the species if Eros keeps getting itself tangled up with Death?

Antigone serves the natural law not by accepting death if that is what is required in order to uphold and respect the natural law, but through the eager embrace of death as though it were her lover, able to erase her pain and humiliation, while reuniting her with her family, with which she is perversely (but nonetheless humanly and humanely) close. What sort of natural law welcomes death as bridegroom and savior, especially when doing so requires that she ignore the reality of her fiancé (who ends up killing himself in frustrated rage after he fails to kill his father, Creon) as well as her sister, both of whom love and care for Antigone? Like the rest of us, Antigone will soon enough spend the dark night of eternity with death. Why the rush?

Nor have I yet mentioned the most infamous and problematic lines of the play, lines some cannot let themselves believe are genuine, though Aristotle quotes from them in his *Rhetoric* (book 3, c. 16) as an example of the persuasive introduction of cause when an assertion appears incredible. Had her son or husband been left unburied, says Antigone, she would not have defied the civic law. Instead, she would have had another child, or married another husband. Only a brother was impossible for her to replace.

> Had I had children or their father dead,
> I'd let them moulder. I should not have chosen
> In such a case to cross the state's decree . . .
> One husband gone, I might have found another,
> Or a child from a new man in first child's place.
> But with my parents hid away in death,
> No brother, ever, could spring up for me.
> Such was the law by which I honored you. (905–915)[7]

Antigone is not operating in the world of natural law as it is normally understood, standing up for universal principles even at the cost of her life. On the contrary, she is enmeshed in the deepest and darkest of particulars, wound tighter and tighter in a net of human love and incest that creates a reality without normal boundaries and limits. Perhaps that is indeed why she can see the natural law when no one else can. And yet we must be honest and say that her perception is perverse: to die for a brother, but not for a son or husband (nor for both together, for she tells us she would have another child by another man), is not a principle of the natural law, but a consequence of her enmeshment in a now mostly dead family she would sooner join than live in the light

---

[7] Other reasons are suggested in *Oedipus at Colonus*. Though the dramatic date is a year or so earlier, the play was produced about forty years later than *Antigone*, when Sophocles was an old man. This is one reason they do not seem relevant here. See especially lines 1250ff.

a little longer. This everyday world with two limited but real human beings who love her holds no attraction whatsoever.

Antigone observes the natural law out of the promptings of dark Eros, as I have called it, a mixture of Eros and Death, a love that seems to seek fusion with the dead. Not just as release from the burden of living, but because fusion with the dead is living. To be sure, one can read *Antigone* as all about the confusion of boundaries, Antigone's father at once her brother, her Uncle Creon confusing being and nonbeing, life with death, to say nothing of his complete and total misunderstanding of the limits of politics vis-à-vis the realm of the gods. Only when everyone he has ever cared about is destroyed does he learn.

Antigone never learns, and while one could argue this is simply because she dies too soon, that is not the answer. Antigone has nothing to learn. She alone of all the characters is not confused about boundaries. Dark Eros is her aim, the love of death deeper and more satisfying than the love of life, as it brings with it an obliterating fusion unavailable to the living. "My life died long ago. And that has made me fit to help the dead" (559–560). This is what motivates Antigone, a woman about whom we should think twice before we proclaim her as a heroine of natural law. For the rest of the characters, confusion comes closer to the mark.

Is it any wonder that in the last extended choral ode of the play, the chorus calls upon Dionysos, Bacchus, whose home is Thebes, the dramatic location of the play, to come home and straighten things out. As if they were calling upon a whirlwind to restore order. Dionysos is the god of a thousand faces, the god of reversal, confusion, and blurring of boundaries, to say nothing of the darker rumors associated with him, including cannibalism. To call upon Dionysos to straighten things out is not so much a measure of desperation as it is a sign that there is nothing left to be straightened out. The forces of Death will have to have their way until they are exhausted, which is precisely what happens.

NATURAL LAW AND NATURAL EVIL

Those who have chosen Antigone as the heroine of natural law (and Maritain is hardly alone) have chosen better than they know. Unwittingly, they have grasped how close natural law comes to natural evil, by which I mean how close love comes to hate, Eros to Death, good to evil, natural law to natural evil.

Does this make Steiner's interpretation of Antigone wrong? Yes, for Steiner writes as if the telluric, primordial place from which Antigone knows the natural law, a place in which knowledge and action are one, is a place of "loving immediacy," and "unquestioning care," which embodies an "imperative of humaneness which men and women share before they enter into the mutations, the transitory illusion, the divisive experiments of a historical and political system" (Steiner 1986, 250–251).

True enough, but that place is not just that place. It is also a place of dark Eros and confusion, of a love that seeks its solace in death, of a love that would prefer the certainty of fusion with death to the uncertainty of human attachments. And, let us not forget, it is a place of rage and hatred easily enough confused with love. "Antígona Furiosa" is an apt name for the Antigone who resides in this telluric place, buried underground, the same place the Furies come to reside in Aeschylus' *Oresteia*, the only place they can reside, lest in their insane hatred they forget the law they are placed under, indeed must be placed under if civilization is to be possible. This is, of course, the theme of Aeschylus' *Oresteia*.

Like all of us, Antigone is filled with rage and hatred as well as love. Given the circumstances of her incestuous birth, she is perhaps even more likely to confuse love and hate, life and death, and in so doing pursue hate and destruction as though the rigidity and rigor of death were signs of life, comparing herself to Tantalus' daughter, turned to stone so that she might cry forever as the rain drips down her rocky cheeks (825–830). Rock is telluric, part of the earth.

Earlier I argued that about the most basic of distinctions, life and death, being and nonbeing, everyone is confused but Antigone, who would choose death over life in a state of utter clarity. But perhaps it is not so simple. As the chorus puts it, "The bad becomes the good to him a god would doom" (621–622). The passage itself is in quotes, indicating that it is no new insight, but already a cliché of the culture. Antigone's certainty is no guarantee she has it right, only that her understanding has become petrified, and her sister knows it.

In Walter Hasenclever's 1917 version of *Antigone*, the author has Ismene say to her sister

> Old injustice is not brought low by new;
> Senselessly you stir to life eternal sorrow...
> Be human among humans!

Be human among humans. It's good advice, based upon Ismene's deep insight into Antigone's motives: not just that she loves her unburied brother Polyneices, but that "you hate Creon, daughter of Oedipus!" (Steiner 1986, 146). Perhaps Antigone, like Clytemnestra, another woman who consorts with Furies, considers herself the rightful heir to the throne.

Death, confusion, dark Eros, fusion with death as though it were life and love, even the love of destruction, but above all confusion of life and death (even when it seems like clarity), exaggerated by incest, the breaking of the most primordial of boundaries: all come from that universal place from which Antigone knows the natural law, that universal place that opposes the polis. It is that same primal place that is the origin of the themes of almost all the Greek tragedies, the themes of generations of hatred, murder, dismemberment, and incest, primal private acts that spill over to confuse and contaminate the public, rather than protect it under the aegis of the natural law.

The place from which Antigone gains access to the natural law is not filled with light, but darkness, a place in which life and death, love and hate, being and nonbeing are soulmates. This place is dangerous but unavoidable, not a place we can or should stay away from, but one that we should enter with both eyes open, for it is a place where death comes too close to life. One might argue that it is a place that needs to be civilized, except that it can't be civilized. Hence, its virtue (that is, its power), and its danger. But that place can be encircled, framed and formed, contained and limited, primarily through the art of conversation, the language of the community. But also through narrative. Greek tragedy was both, a celebration of community and a narrative that warned of Furies hiding just below the surface. This is seen most clearly, perhaps, in Aeschylus' *Oresteia* trilogy, but the contemporary playwright who titled her play "Antígona Furiosa" knew what she was talking about.

What is a civilized community to do with its Furies? This is the question addressed by almost all of the Greek tragedies (that Euripides transformed the Furies into the spiteful insanity of mere men and women, as in *Orestes*, only makes his plays less auratic). And it is the question that should be – but generally isn't – addressed by natural law, though Saint Augustine came close for a moment. What I call reparative natural law comes closer still, recognizing that life is always just a narrow victory away from death. The purpose of reparative natural law is to allow us to frame and form this encounter with death, so that we might know it without falling victim to it, or becoming confused by this encounter – that is, without becoming too much like Antigone, or Creon.

Confusion of good and bad, life and death, Eros and Thanatos (the name Karl Jung gave to the *Todestrieb*), is the usual way in which death is defended against if we lack the frame and form of a story, a metanarrative if you will, to make sense of our encounter. For all the reasons yet to be given, reparative natural law is one of the best stories around. Not just because it is a good story, though that's important, but because it fits our human nature, that other reviled term these days. But the idea of human nature need not be reviled, not if we understand human nature as itself one more story. *Antigone* is a good beginning.

The next chapter is not much concerned with dark Eros. Instead, it is based on interviews with thirty informants on questions about the natural law. Rather than taking up the *Todestreib*, it takes up the issue raised by MacIntyre contra Steiner. How does one come to know the natural law? Is the individualism of advanced modernity such that the natural law is no longer available to most people? Community has almost vanished, and the telluric experience to which Steiner refers (even were it not an idealization) seems no longer available to those tuned in to iPods and cell phones. But perhaps community and telluric experience are not the only ways in which people know the natural law. Maybe people just feel it, the result of an experience of shared humanity not so readily enunciated or eradicated.

2

Young People, Relativism, and the Natural Law

Based on my research – hour long interviews with thirty young people – I uncovered no yearning for dark Eros. To do so would require hours of in-depth psychological research with each subject, and besides the interview room is not the right place to look. Look at Abu Grabe. Read the history of the twentieth century, the bloodiest in world history, over 100 million killed in armed conflict, over 170 million if one includes "democide," such as the 40 million (or more) Russian deaths ordered by Stalin. Does not, Freud wondered, every human long for death? First one seeks the death of others. Young men march off to war; the rest of us read about it excitedly in the newspapers (Freud 1915). Old men and women seek their own death (even as most think they are postponing it, if they think about it at all), as though the goal of life itself were silence, sleep, night, death – the cessation of all stimulation. This is the thesis of the *Todestrieb*, the death drive posited by Freud (1920) in order to explain the longing for stasis that seems to lie beyond the pleasure principle.

What I wanted to discover and explain was something quite different. Not the presence of Antigone's dark Eros in each of us, but something far more superficial, indeed banal: the relativism of the young that MacIntyre (2000), Alan Bloom (1988), and Russell Hittinger (2003), among many others have asserted, a relativism that makes natural law, including reparative natural law, irrelevant. As Bloom put it about his undergraduates at the University of Chicago, they are convinced of only two things – that the truth is relative and that everyone

23

is equal. Furthermore, these two beliefs are related: only if the truth is relative, one truth as good as another, does equality among those with diverse beliefs make sense. Democracy itself is built on relativism. That other grounds of toleration might be found does not seem to enter the heads of Bloom's undergraduates, or so he tells us (1988, 25). A disturbing experience of my own, about which I will tell you in a moment, confirmed these scholars' views, and so I set out to better understand the relativism of the young. In fact, I discovered something quite different: little relativism and a widespread belief in a minimal version of the natural law. This, though, was not quite as reassuring as it might sound.

Reparative natural law, loosely derived from (or perhaps I should just say inspired by) the work of Melanie Klein is first of all an instance of natural law: that means that it is teleologically oriented, based upon a developmental ideal. Or as Michael Rustin (1991, 147–149) puts it in *The Good Society and the Inner World,* an

aspect of Kleinian thinking, which, I shall argue, had significant social affinities was its teleological dimension. There is inherent in Kleinian theory the idea of a 'normal' pathway of development . . . The 'depressive position' defined as a state of affairs that was normative . . . was held in some way to correspond to the potential of human nature.

With the term "depressive position," Klein refers not to what is ordinarily called depression, but to an awareness of how much one has hated as well as loved, how much one has longed to destroy as well as create. I will explore this theme in the next chapter.

For now, the key point is that reparative natural law gets no special exemption from the traditional demands placed upon the natural law. If young people really are relativists (whatever that means; the term is ambiguous, as we shall see), then reparative natural law will have little to say to them, even if the natural law remains true in a more abstract sense. If so, reparative natural law will have to wait for another time, place, and generation for its truths to be appreciated.

There is another way to think about this chapter: that it takes up, and in the end falsifies, MacIntyre's claim that unlike ancient Greek culture, as well as the communitarian culture of the Middle Ages, the individualistic culture of advanced modernity cannot support the natural law. The next two chapters take up Steiner's sanguine characterization of that telluric place where Antigone encountered the natural law.

A DISTURBING EXPERIENCE

The inspiration for my research goes back a number of years, when I was invited to be a member of a committee charged with developing a new ethics curriculum to be taught in the county schools. On the committee were a minister, priest, and rabbi, several concerned parents, and me. We met in the conference room of the local school board, which was moderately impressive, sitting in the same chairs the school board members sat in. Other than the ghostly presence of the school board, we were on our own.

We began with elementary school students. What should they be taught? General principles were easy enough to agree on, such as "treat other students with respect." What got difficult was when we got down to practice, such as "students shouldn't hit each other."

"Some cultures value the physical expression of difference," said one committee member.

"Who are we to say otherwise?" added another.

And so it went with this odd conversation. Odd not just because of the extreme cultural relativism, but because not a single member of the ethics committee thought children should hit each other. Quite the contrary; all were against it. Not only that, but no one could name any actual culture in which students hitting each other was deemed a good thing. It was the very possibility that some culture, somewhere might value the physical expression of difference that stymied most members of the committee.

The committee members had lost (presumably they never had) confidence in their own ability to judge right from wrong, though this puts it a little too simply. They themselves were in no doubt about whether children should hit each other. All were against it. But most believed they had no grounds to say something so clear and concrete. This included the minister, the priest, and the rabbi, all of whom said that according to their religious beliefs it was of course wrong for students to hit each other, but none wished to impose their religious beliefs on others. In our modern world, morality has been defeated by epistemology, or is it just sociology?

One might see the committee members as MacIntyre (2000) would, victims of the culture of advanced modernity, unable to understand themselves as engaged in a cooperative attempt to discover, practice, and teach the human good to themselves and the next generation. Not because they don't know the good, but because they doubted their right to teach their beliefs to others, as democracy itself seems to rest on this doubt – that is, on relativism. This, of course, is Bloom's (1988, 25) point. Absent an official relativism, it is a straight line to the Taliban, or so many people seem to believe.

Is this because the committee members believed that their views were no more than an unjustifiable personal preference, akin to preferring chocolate ice cream over vanilla? No, most believed that it was right and good to teach children not to hit each other. They were simply unable to articulate the grounds of their belief in a language that might convince the mythical relativist, as though this were the real problem, as though epistemology were the devil who bedevils ethics. Not their own relativism, but their lack of confidence in their ability to justify their moral beliefs and commitments in a common human language held the committee members in thrall. No example of such a language, such as natural law, existed for any of the committee members, not even the religious leaders, who were profoundly (one might say overly) aware that they were citizens of a secular culture.

Almost a decade later, when I turned my attention to younger men and women, I mistakenly believed that I would discover the demoralization that characterized the ethics committee, come to full bloom. Like the ethics committee, only more so, they would be stymied, unable to make the simplest moral judgment. This is not what I found.

What I found was at first glance similar to the situation described by MacIntyre in the opening pages of *After Virtue* (1981, 1–3). Imagine that an ecological catastrophe occurred, brought on by the unfettered experimentation of scientists. Angry mobs burned laboratories, as well as libraries filled with scientific journals. Much later, at least a generation, possibly more, scholars as well as ordinary men and women would try to reconstruct the science that had been lost. They would recover many of the terms, such as "molecule," or "inertia," but the experimental and theoretical framework that gave these terms meaning was lost. Neither the ideal of the scientific method, nor the theories in which these terms were embedded, and which gave them meaning, was available to the new scientists. As a result, their use of scientific terms was arbitrary, and ultimately incoherent.

This is the situation with ethics today, says MacIntyre. Terms like morally right, even "the human good" remain, but the context, which is roughly that of the Aristotelian world view, in which the goal of a good human life was obvious for all to see, has disappeared. Absent, in other words, is the evaluative framework, the good for man and woman, which makes a judgment about a life more than a matter of taste. Where once one could talk about a human life as one might talk about a watch, measuring each by objectively shared standards of excellence, that time has long passed. Today it's all a matter of taste and choice.

At first I thought that this is what I was hearing from the young people I interviewed, but I was mistaken. "Informants" I call these young people, using the anthropological term, for that is what I came to feel I was doing, studying the beliefs of a strange new culture, one with hidden depths, as well as stunning superficialities, neither of which I suspected, even as I live daily among its members. An appendix to this chapter contains the questions I asked and more information about the interviews.

WHAT INFORMANTS SAID

Thirty young people ages nineteen to twenty-eight were my informants, almost equally divided between men and women. Hardly a random sample, they were nonetheless diverse, holding half a dozen different religious beliefs, with family connections all over the globe. Almost one-fourth were first generation Americans – that is, the first generation of their family to be born and bred in America. More nonwhites than in a strictly random sample were interviewed. Though my sample size is too small to draw any conclusions, it is not my impression that race or religion made the slightest difference in how informants answered the questions. What did seem to make a difference for several informants was being raised by parents with continuing strong ties to traditional Asian, African, or South American cultures. Overall, however, it is the similarity in the beliefs of this demographically diverse group of young people that is most striking. Being born and bred in America is by far the most important variable of all.

Unlike the ethics committee, informants were not intimidated by relativism. On the contrary, most held quite definite beliefs about right and wrong; furthermore, they regarded these beliefs as binding on others as well as themselves. Only one informant said anything like Rita. "For me, abortion isn't just wrong. It's murder. But that's only my opinion." That is, only one informant made a universal moral claim in one breath, and in the next qualified it as pertaining only to herself, a mere opinion. Hers was a position as incoherent as that described by MacIntyre, where the language of universal principles is used to express what are in fact personal preferences. Or is it vice-versa? For Rita there was no difference.

Informants' moral views were not always crystal clear. They were, however, almost always expressed in the form of a coherent narrative, a story about the conditions of a decent human life, albeit not an excellent one. To be sure, the story told by most informants had the quality of a radically simplified narrative, one in which most of the details are glossed, so that it reads more like a plot outline than a story. But a plot outline is not incoherent, just something that needs to be filled in. How that might work is addressed along the way.

In one respect my approach was straightforward, in another not. The questions I asked were ones to which I really wanted to know the answers. In that sense my approach was straightforward. What was not quite so straightforward was my focus on the moral reasoning involved.

Why do you think that way?

What has led you to that conclusion?

What if I don't accept your assumption, is there any way you could persuade me?

Not everyone thinks the way you do. How is it you came to this particular conclusion?

What if I were to say that's a really strange opinion? How would you respond?

It is with follow-up questions like these that I tried to get at the reasoning involved, and ultimately to find the informant's stopping place, beyond which he or she could not go without falling into incoherence or silence. One way or another I kept asking "why?" This meant that I pushed a little harder than I was comfortable with, harder than I have in other interviews for other research projects. Still, none of the informants seemed to get angry, or become agitated. Perhaps this is because we were talking about an issue, and using examples, that were not terribly close to the heart of most informants.

I expected informants to stop either at God (that is, sacred scrip-ture) or "sociological relativism." When pressed by a series of "why" questions about morality, I expected them either to rest their argument on an ultimate authority, God, or the opposite, such as the informant who said "that's just how we do things in our culture." This informant was, however, not the norm. Indeed, my expectations were met nei-ther about God nor relativism, though one could argue that the "social contract," a common answer, is a version of sociological relativism.

This, though, is not how most informants talked about the social contract. For most of those who referred or alluded to the social con-tract (in one way or another, almost eighty percent), the social contract is rooted in what I call "metaphysical biology." As one informant put it, "we are all born in the same way, we all came from the same place," so that makes everybody equal.

Actually, Robert said "that makes everybody the same." It is I who translated "the same" into "equal," and not without some difficulty.

Do you mean everyone is identical, I asked?

"No, of course not. I mean that because we all come from the same place we are all the same."

"Oh, you mean that we all have the same basic human rights," I said.

"Not exactly. That's the way you put it in the language professors use. I mean something simpler than that. I don't know how to put it into your words. I mean that about some things we really *are* the same. Not about baseball and grades, things like that, but about life."

Though I continued to ask Robert questions, I never got any closer to what he really meant. One possibility is that he could not articulate what he really meant. The other was that he could articulate what he really meant, and this was it. In the end I was never quite sure with Robert.

Robert was an exception, but he was not the lone exception. If the natural law has the qualities attributed to it by Maritain (2001, 34–35), a "melody produced by the vibration of deep-rooted tendencies made present in the subject," then imprecision is something we must accept. Natural law never was a law or precept to begin with; that comes much later, the product of schoolmen and lawyers. The problem is that melodies are open to interpretation, both by the interviewer, and the subject. But, there seems to be no alternative. I will try state when I am doing more than the usual amount of interpreting.

Robert's position was shared by most informants, even as they themselves were generally the ones to conclude "so that makes us equal"
(or some similar phrase) without any prompting. I call this position
metaphysical biology because a biological fact, that we are all born in
the same way, is seen as the ground of an ethical claim. More precisely
put, for most informants, biological fact *is* an ethical claim; there is no
gulf between "is" and "ought" to be bridged. Metaphysical biology *is*
natural law, albeit a radically simplified version.

Why not lie, cheat, or steal I asked? (The burden of several questions.)

"Because if everybody did that, there would be no society left. Society
is based on a contract. Without rules there would be nothing," is how
Don put it.

Sam put it a little differently. "From kindergarten on, everyone
learns the rules of life. Play fair, don't cheat, don't steal. Most people don't even think about it, but when you do, you see that it's like
we were all born into the same club. You get to join just by being a
member of the human race, but you only get to stay a member if you
play by the rules. Most people want to belong, and even if they don't,
they're too scared not to."

Joyce explained the social contract this way. "No one ever says 'sign
this piece of paper and you can belong to society.' But that's the way
it works. With millions of people you have to have rules."

Do the rules make sense, I asked?

"Usually they do, but it doesn't really matter. Having the rules is
more important than agreeing with every little detail."

Why, I asked?

"Because without rules no one would know what to expect. Even
though some drivers run red lights, most don't, and that means I can
get where I'm going without getting killed."

Have you ever run a red light, I asked?

"Once or twice, when I was really in a hurry, but usually I don't."

Because you're afraid of getting a ticket, I asked?

"No, not just that. It's just the way the game is played. If you want to
play, you have to have rules. Otherwise you get hurt or killed. . . . When
my mom was a kid they used to have a game called 'Life.' She
made me and my sisters play it with her when we were kids, like it
was a big treat. [Joyce rolls her eyes.] Well, that was just a game.

What we are talking about now, that's the real rules of the game of life."

If one were going to characterize the view of most informants, positivistic natural law would seem to come closest to the mark. The preeminent theorist of positivistic natural law is H. L. A. Hart (1994). Given certain facts of human nature, Hart argues that enforceable law is necessary if humans are to live decently among each other. The facts of human nature include the following:

Human vulnerability: if humans had exoskeletons, natural law would look quite different.

Relative equality: the weakest can kill the strongest because even the strong must sleep.

Limited altruism: people are not devils, but neither are they angels.

Limited resources: people need food and shelter, and so some institution of property, though not necessarily private property, is needed.

Limited understanding and strength of will: most can see the point of this minimal natural law (for that is what Hart calls it), but frequently lack the foresight and strength of will to stick to these arrangements (Hart 1994, 194–198).

Given these facts, says Hart, one can see that the laws of states and nations, what is called positive law, are rooted in natural necessity, which Hart readily characterizes with the term natural law. "These simple truisms we have discussed . . . disclose the core of good sense in the doctrine of Natural Law" (199).

Trouble is, the natural necessity to which Hart refers is void of moral content. An unjust legal system would fulfill the needs of stability as well as a just legal system. A system of laws that preserved the security, stability, and property of its members would be valid, even if these laws condoned slavery and the persecution of minorities. One thinks here of National Socialism in Germany, a system of obsessive legality, under which the dispossession and persecution of the Jews was perfectly legal.

Hart recognizes this problem. He simply doesn't think it is best solved under the guidance of the natural law. On the contrary, men and women must take the moral burden upon themselves to violate an iniquitous law, as Hart calls it (1994, 211–212). Hart holds this position because he believes that "the *minimum content* of Natural Law" is supported by the facts of human nature, whereas "a teleological conception of nature as containing in itself levels of excellence" is "too metaphysical for modern minds" (1994, 192–193, emphasis his).

Hart quite properly does not imagine that the naturalistic fallacy (the so-called derivation of "ought" from "is") poses a barrier to natural law. If it did, the barrier would operate at every level of the natural law, including Hart's own. There is no reason that humans "ought" to survive.[1] Where Hart goes wrong, or at least provides insufficient guidance, especially in light of the experience of informants, is in implying that in stepping outside the law one is stepping into a realm of moral nothingness, or at least into a realm in which nothing useful can be said. Hart does not state this explicitly, but because he says nothing else about this realm outside the law, that is the conclusion one must draw. The complement of Hart's positivistic natural law is moral decisionism. I return to this point shortly.

Freud said that neurotics, and many others besides, "take exception to the fact that '*inter urinas et faeces nascimur* [we are born between urine and faeces]'" (Freud 1930, 108).

Informants are neither this graphic, nor quite this reductive. Yet, far from objecting to this fact, almost half of informants referred in one way or another to the physical facts of birth or death as conveying moral as well as legal equality. "We all enter the world the same way, and we leave in the same way too," says John.

What's that mean, I asked?

"It means that we are all equal."

Do you mean physically the same, I replied?

"I mean we all deserve to be treated equally," replied John in a tone that suggested I just didn't get it.

Some informants used the "language professors use" more fluently than others. Whether this means that this language came closer to their actual experience of the natural law is quite another question. My prejudice was that Robert's apparent inarticulateness came closer to a genuine and intense experience of the natural law than John's, but it's probably not so simple. About abstract feelings of identification with other humans, for that is the aspect of the natural law we are

---

[1] The objections raised by Hume and others, and often grouped under the "naturalistic fallacy" are not done away with so easily. They are addressed at length toward the conclusion of Chapter 4.

talking about just now, there is no reason to be less impressed with fluid and facile formulations than inarticulate and stubborn ones. What is clear is that while the *content* of informants' vision of the natural law is similar to Hart's, and in this respect is quite limited, informants hold the natural law on grounds quite different from that of Hart.

Not sociological relativism, and not God, but a version of natural law thinking based on biological commonality grounds a basic set of human rights that almost all informants share: they want these rights for themselves, and they recognize that others, so similar to themselves as far as the basics are concerned, possess these rights as well (though this last point gets a little complicated, as we shall see). Or as King Solomon put it,

When I was born, I breathed the common air, and was laid on the earth that all men tread: and the first sound I uttered, as all do, was a cry ... There is no king that had any other beginning; for all come into life by a single path, and by a single path go out again. (Wisdom of Solomon, 7:3–6)

Morris expressed a similar idea, albeit less elegantly, when he said "we're born, we live, we die, and along the way we try to be happy?"

Does everyone have a right to be happy?"

"Yes, but that doesn't mean that everyone gets to be happy. That depends on luck and how hard you work. Mostly luck, like not being born in Iraq."

I must have looked surprised, even shocked, that someone would be quite so crass. The result was that Morris began to elaborate about "the natural right of every man, woman and child to be free to follow ... [and so on and so forth]." But I think we both knew that he'd said what he meant, and that everything that followed his comment about Iraq was embellishment. Anyway, I wasn't offended, just surprised. I needed to work on my poker face.

Like Hart, informants hold to the minimum content of natural law. Unlike Hart, they make no distinction between what is contingently necessary to hold society together and what men and women ought to do. For informants, is and ought flow into each other as readily as the Tigris and Euphrates, but only about those practices that make civilization possible. Unlike Aquinas, as well as so many other theorists of the natural law, informants do not go on to "deduce," or (as I have argued) tell a story about the development or evolution of this confluence in history, or contemporary experience. On the contrary, a number of informants who believe in the minimal natural law went on to say that they would cheat on a test, or even a government contract, if doing so meant the difference between passing and failing, keeping the job or getting fired. The minimal natural law is just that: minimal. It does not extend to or imply practices such as honesty, trustworthiness, commitment to community, love of justice, and so forth, at least not when issues of life and death are not involved.

For Thomas Aquinas, paradigmatic theorist of the natural law, natural law is the way in which humans participate in the Eternal Law, which is God's law, the reason of the Ruler of the Universe (ST I–II, 91).[2] Yet, good Aristotelian that he is, Aquinas argues that because natural law is in accord with tutored human nature, not contrary to it, one can know the natural law and act in accord with it simply by being brought up in a decent human community. Or as Hugo Grotius (orig. 1625) put it four centuries later,

What we have been saying [about natural law] would have a degree of validity even if we should concede that which cannot be conceded without the utmost wickedness, that there is no God, or that the affairs of men are of no concern to Him. (Grotius 1964, Prolegomena, II)

---

[2] The *Stanford Encyclopedia of Philosophy* (plato.stanford.edu) puts it plainly in its entry on "The Natural Law Tradition in Ethics." "If any moral theory is a theory of natural law, it is Aquinas's." Yet, it would be mistaken to hold that Aquinas is the first natural law theorist. One might award that status to Aristotle, who cites Antigone's speech (line 456) invoking gods' law over man's in support of the existence of eternal laws. Only it turns out that Aristotle is giving advice to defense lawyers whose clients have broken the civil law! (*Rhetoric*, bk 1, c. 15). While one can find other statements in Aristotle suggestive of the natural law (*N. Ethics*, 1134b18–1135a4), the true founder of the natural law is surely Marcus Tullius Cicero. In *On the Republic*, Cicero states that

True law is right reason conformable to nature, universal, unchangeable, eternal, whose commands urge us to duty, and whose prohibitions restrain us from evil.... This law cannot be contradicted by any other law, and is not liable either to derogation or abrogation.... It needs no other expositor and interpreter than our own conscience. It is not one thing at Rome, and another at Athens; one thing today and another tomorrow, but in all times and nations this universal law must forever reign, eternal and imperishable. It is the sovereign master and emperor of all beings. God himself is its author...and he who does not obey it flies from himself, and does violence to the very nature of man. (III, 22)

What clearer statement of the traditional natural law could there be than that?

For Aquinas, the founding principle of the natural law is deceptively simple: "good is to be done, and evil is to be avoided" (ST I–II, 94, 2).[3] From this single assumption Aquinas infers a wide range of duties that are at the same time natural inclinations (*inclinationum naturalium*). For Aquinas, duty generally works with rather than against nature. These inclinations include procreating and caring for children, as well as shunning ignorance (*ignorantiam vitet*) and fostering community in general. Later I will suggest that these last two inclinations go together, that the type of knowledge, indeed the concept of reason, to which Aquinas refers, has little to do with the Reason of the Enlightenment. For Aquinas, "the pursuit of knowledge and sociability . . . might be interpreted minimally as social consciousness, maximally as love" (Kainz 2004, 22). Not only his focus on fostering life, but his conception of knowledge and reason as modes of social relatedness, bring Aquinas closer to Klein and Bion than one would otherwise expect.[4]

For most informants, the natural law implies only itself. One should not lie, cheat, or steal if that is going to cost another person his life, liberty, or large amounts of his property. But if the result is that the

---

[3] Some scholars, particularly the new natural law theorists as they are called, argue that Aquinas' founding principle, "do good, avoid evil," is little more than a tautology. These considerations need not detain us, though we shall return to them. *Natural Law and Natural Rights* by John Finnis (1980) and *In Defense of Natural Law* by Robert George (1999), are exemplary works of the new natural law.

[4] Leo Strauss (1999, 139–159) makes quite the opposite argument, holding that Thomas' (ST I–I 79, 12) account of how the principles of natural law are originally impressed on conscience (*synderesis*) through a direct experience of the beauty of nature

leaves scant room for reflective consideration of past experience or practical exigencies, no room at all for discursive deliberation in which the wisdom of others might be sifted and weighted, and no time for prudential self-assessment or inner critique. (Schneck 2004, 19)

Though I will not be taking up Strauss's argument again, my argument in the coming chapters assumes that our knowledge of basic goods for Thomas is profoundly social because basic goods themselves are social, shared with others, indeed conceivable only as shared experience. For example, one could never learn what the good of preserving community means without years of experience living in a community. Indeed, one could never learn this good without being able to share in the experience of generations who have passed this good down to us as culture and institutions. Not just how one learns, but the content of what is learned, makes a difference in assessing whether it is "discursive." Or rather, some things are only learned in a discursive manner, no matter how one characterizes the original encounter with the first principle.

liar gets better grades and a better job, so be it. Not every informant concluded in this way, but a surprising number did.

Why? Because metaphysical biology is quite literally superficial, concerning only the basics we share as embodied humans. Metaphysical biology is deficient in the teleological structure that has traditionally defined natural law, and almost totally lacking in the complex narrative structure that has taken the place of teleology in the work of MacIntyre and others. Jacques Maritain (2001, 29) exemplifies both traditions when he calls the natural law "the ideal formula of development of a given being." In other words, natural law doesn't just characterize what we have in common, but what we *could* have in common if we were all to develop ourselves as perfectly and completely as possible. Klein characterizes this complete development in terms of the depressive position. The traditional natural law uses a different vocabulary and concepts, but both contain a developmental ideal.

Metaphysical biology, on the other hand, while having a teleological structure – to be born is to share equally and naturally in the goods of life, liberty, and security – gets stuck at the beginning, evidently because it is so biological, so body-based. In this respect, metaphysical biology comes close to Hobbes's account of the fear of violent death that unites us all under the sovereign. Hobbes (*Leviathan*, part 1, c's 14–15) understands his account in *Leviathan* as being entirely in accord with the natural law, and others, such as Norberto Bobbio (1993), have interpreted Hobbes in this vein. But it is a vein that runs no deeper, and more importantly can run no deeper, than Hart's positivistic natural law. That is, no deeper than the metaphysical biology of most informants.

What about the significant minority of informants who, when pushed, did not invoke metaphysical biology as the final answer to my series of "why" questions? Instead, most of these responded as the new natural law theorists respond. If someone hasn't already figured out that everyone is better off when all subscribe to the social contract, then further argument is unlikely to convince them. In other words, a significant minority of informants treat the social contract as a basic good in itself, the term the new natural law theorists, such as John Finnis (1980) and Robert George (1992, 37) use to refer to something whose goodness does not need to be explained or argued for, such as health. All simply agree that health is a good in itself, much as Aristotle argued that happiness is an end in itself (*N. Ethics* 1102a).

Similarly, one can enumerate the reasons that the social contract is good for all concerned, but if someone just doesn't get it, there is probably not much else to be said or done. "The next steps are shunning, ostracism, and jail," as one informant put it. Robert George puts the argument this way:

> Still, someone might object: is there not something unsatisfying about appeals to self-evidence even at the level of the most basic premises of moral arguments? After all, people can simply refuse to accept a claim that something is self-evident.... It seems to me that ... appeals to self-evidence, when properly understood, do not fail to provide a solid foundation for moral reasoning. In any event, they provide no less solid a foundation than appeals to the facts of human nature.... Someone who finds it baffling that anyone would pursue friendship just for friendship's sake is unlikely to understand the value of friendship any better by being informed (or even persuaded) that man is by nature a social being. (1992, 37)

Interesting about the self-evidence of the social contract is that not a single informant thought that the "defect strategy," as it is called in game theory, was worth arguing against, and not because they assumed it in advance. They just didn't think that way. What would happen, I asked, if someone said in effect "let everybody else obey the social contract; that just means more opportunity for me to lie, cheat, and steal?" (This question is implicit in several questions, and explicit in question 9; see appendix.) This is the position of Plato's Thrasymachus (*Republic* 336b–354b), and it is why Hobbes thought a mighty sovereign was necessary.

Informants who saw the social contract as self-evident didn't talk this way. Since most were more than willing to indulge their selfishness about other matters, I have no reason to think they were misleading me or themselves. In this regard, informants fail to fulfill MacIntyre's (2000) assumption that the culture of advanced modernity is one of extreme individualism. For game theory (even so-called cooperative games, such as the famous prisoner's dilemma) assumes that the individual always puts him or herself first. About the minimal content of natural law, as Hart calls it, most informants were willing to see themselves as equals.

"Most people are socialized to play by the rules, and those who aren't will one day pay the price," said Joan. "And even if a few don't, most still play by the rules, and that's enough."

Do people like to play by the rules, I asked?

"It's not a matter of like or dislike. It's the way people are brought up."

Do you think it's natural to want to play by the rules?

"What's natural?" Joan replied. "It's whatever you want to do, that's what's natural, and most people either want to play by the rules or are too scared not to, and that's enough to keep society going."

The self-evident social contract theorists among informants (as I will call them when distinguishing between them and the metaphysical biologists, who also hold to the social contract, but for somewhat different reasons) appear to express a morality that stands closer to the traditional natural law. The self-evident social contract theorists conceive of individuals as fundamentally social, oriented toward reciprocity, and bound by something like the Golden Rule: if I benefit from the social contract, I will want to play by the same rules. This way of putting it invokes more of the language or spirit of the traditional natural law as it is usually formulated. Humanity, says Aquinas, has a natural inclination "to live in society: and in this respect, whatever pertains to this inclination belongs to the natural law; for instance ... to avoid offending those among whom one has to live" (ST I–II, 94).

In fact, I don't think there is much difference except perspective, or rather the distance of imagination. The strict metaphysical biologists ("we all come from the same place") are positing an abstract, imaginary human community, one that reflects and creates obligations among us all, albeit within fairly narrow limits. The strict social contract theorists, those who see the contract in the here and now, are in a certain sense less imaginative, but probably slightly more social, willing to consider a slightly wider set of obligations as falling under the contract. Why this is so I am not certain. I hypothesize that even though it is based upon a particularly concrete, body-based ideal, the metaphysical social contract is first of all an idea, originating in an act of imagination, not in everyday practice. In other words, metaphysical biology is more distant from practice than its content alone would suggest.

Finally, I should note that the distinction between metaphysical biologists and strict social contract theorists is really a continuum.

I can place about a dozen informants at the metaphysical end, not quite half a dozen at the strict social contract end. Almost all the rest, like Sam (who used kindergarten as his model), fall somewhere in between. Not included are those few (four or five) who expressed quite a different orientation, the care perspective, discussed shortly. A couple of informants' views I couldn't place at all.

In any case, there were virtually no relativists among informants (there was one). I encountered little of the doubt that I experienced as a member of the school district's ethics committee. The reasons are complex, but surely one is that for both the metaphysical biologists and self-evident social contract theorists the social contract doesn't go very far. For both groups, the social contract may be compatible with lying and cheating to get ahead (though not with hitting other students!).

"I believe in the social contract, and I try to follow it. But if I were really under pressure for the grade or the job, I'd lie or cheat if I had to. I think most people would. The social contract is what keeps civilization going. It's not really about small things. It's about not killing, stuff like that."

I decided to challenge Judith, for I'd been hearing responses like hers for some time, and I was getting suspicious. So I said "What if I replied that I think you are defining the social contract like you do to let yourself off the hook in matters of morality in everyday life? Would I be really mean to say that?"

"No, it wouldn't be mean. It just wouldn't be true," Judith replied, neither holding my gaze nor avoiding it. I think she meant what she said. That is, I think Judith was telling the truth. Her truth, but for the moment that's the only truth we are concerned with.

Consider Raymond, who says that he would "cheat in a minute" in a tough chemistry class if he knew he could get away with it. Nor does he bother to defend his cheating in terms of cheating having become the de facto norm, as other informants did (see question 2). Raymond's reasoning was strictly instrumental. "The cheater gets hired, and you don't, so why not do it. It's an easy advantage to take."

There was something so cold and calculating about Raymond that I couldn't stop asking questions.

Would you steal a good student's notes to get a better grade? I asked.

Again, his answer was instrumental. In a large class (an explicit assumption of my question) nothing would be gained by harming another student, so if he could steal another student's notes, copy them, and give them back, he would.

And if you couldn't return the notes? I asked.

"Well, that would depend on how bad I needed the grade."

Though he was the only informant who gave me the creeps, there was no sadism here, no sense of pleasure in depriving a good student of his semester's work by stealing his notes. Creepy was the absence of these emotions, as though Raymond were an advantage calculating machine. (In my research for another book, I participated in a psychopathy identification project, learning to identify imprisoned psychopaths by interviewing them; Raymond was not even in the minor leagues of psychopathy [Alford 1997].)

Raymond too was a minimal social contract theorist (of the metaphysical biological variety). Life, liberty, and the security of person should be respected because "people everywhere are basically the same." For Raymond this meant that people are enough like me that I can imagine their suffering. He was not untouched by my suggestion that the student who had his class notes stolen might be made anxious and upset. That fact entered into his calculations. It seemed to be the reason he would prefer to copy the notes and return them if he could. But, the fact that people are enough like me to suffer as I do means, for Raymond, they are enough like me that right now they are trying to figure out how to take advantage of me. So I had better figure out how to take advantage of them first, albeit within the limits of the minimal social contract, lest the whole world fall apart.

Most informants were not this bold or this harsh, but they came close. None, by the way, seemed particularly bothered by the minimal character of the social contract. While I sometimes felt they made the contract about such big things so as to be free of morality in everyday life, I was unable to get a single informant to admit this (I tried my "confronting Judith strategy" with half a dozen informants). It remains possible that I am wrong to suspect that informants would make morality about "life, liberty, and security of person" in order to free them from having to judge themselves or others about matters of everyday morality, such as lying and cheating. Or rather, I'm not wrong to suspect this (suspect everything!), but my suspicions are not confirmed by informants "resistance," as the psychoanalysts put it. Of all that I learned interviewing informants, the most important is that theirs was in many respects an alien culture: deeper than I imagined, and shallower too. But mostly different. To assume that informants were acting on motives they denied does not seem like a good policy, at least in the absence of anything more than an older, more educated man's doubts about a younger, less educated, but no less feeling, generation.

CARE AND IMAGINATION ARE MISSING

Missing among most informants is a view of society loosely based on the extended family. To be sure, contract plays a leading role in the modern world, but it is not the alpha and omega of the natural law. The extended family is the framework within which Aquinas viewed the natural law (ST I–II, 94, 4, 6). One sees this in the leading principles of Thomistic natural law.

Preserve human life, and avoid its destruction.

Foster marriage and the sound upbringing of children.

Educate and care for the children.

Preserve community and avoid giving unnecessary offense to others.

Respect private property except in exceptional circumstances, such as when the community is starving, and what food that remains is in the hands of a few speculators who are hoarding it, waiting for prices to go up. Then the community is justified in treating the property of individuals as though it belonged to the entire community, as once it did (ST I–II 94, 2).

While it is hard to disagree with Aquinas, many, such as Reinhold Niebuhr (1988), argue that Thomistic natural law remains inextricably bound to a medieval worldview, while remaining overconfident in reason. For Aquinas, the Fall robbed man of grace, but left him with reason. For Niebuhr, that is too easy. The Fall corrupted reason itself, rendering reason arrogant and self-satisfied. Ours is not an incomplete world yearning for completion. Ours is a tragic world, filled with arrogance, false eternals, and bogus absolutes.

Whether the charges of medievalism and overconfidence in reason fit Thomas, they are certainly not true of Jacques Maritain, once considered socially radical, the "Red Christian." Maritain came to Thomism through Henri Bergson's phenomenology. Though he soon gave up

phenomenology as doctrine and discipline, Maritain always saw the
experience of natural law as akin to intuition, as much about the evo-
cation of feeling as reason.

> Knowledge by inclination or by connaturality is a kind of knowledge that is
> not clear, like that obtained through concepts and conceptual judgments. It
> is obscure, unsystematic, vital knowledge by means of instinct or sympathy,
> and in which the intellect, in order to make its judgments, consults the inner
> leanings of the subject – the experience that he has of himself – and listens
> to the melody produced by the vibration of deep-rooted tendencies made
> present in the subject. (Maritain 2001, 34–35)

Not all would agree with this way of looking at the natural law, and
perhaps we should be careful. Knowledge by inclination is not, as one
of Maritain's defenders misguidedly puts it, "a combination of low-
grade cognitive and affective activity. Sometimes it is close to animal
feeling" (Bourke 1988, 218). Knowledge by inclination is closer to the
knowledge of reality that we gain through art and poetry, which Maritain understands not as mystical insight, but reason subject to the love
of beauty. As another commentator puts it, "given its twentieth century
course, it is Maritain's judgment that poetry has never been in greater
need of reason, of genuine human wisdom.... The allurements of
magic must be counterbalanced by the judgmental character of rational knowledge" (Dougherty 2003, 86; Maritain 1953, 234–235). This is
not just an abstract problem, as my problem interpreting what Robert
meant by "we are all the same" reveals. Was Robert being poetic, or
literal, even frighteningly so?

Whether Maritain is correct in capturing the balance between reason and intuition (connaturality) in Aquinas, I leave for others to
decide. Of course, Maritain could be incorrect about the balance in
Thomas, and still hold a sensible position regarding the relationship
between reason and intuition, as I believe he does. For Maritain, the
natural law runs through us, plucking our heart strings as it makes its
way (Maritain 2001, 34–35).

What could a vague poetic expression like "plucking our heart
strings" mean? It means what great poetry and art have always meant:
that they tell us the truth, with just enough of a nimbus of beauty to
make the truth bearable. "Beauty is nothing but the beginning of terror that we are still just able to bear," says Rilke (*Duino Elegies* 2000,

first elegy). This is what Iris Murdoch means when she says that "the realism of a great artist is not a photographic realism, it is essentially both pity and justice" (Murdoch 1970, 87). Pity and justice not just for the subject, she might have added, but for the human race.

The part about justice and the natural law is fairly straightforward. What about the pity? Pity (*misericordia*), I will argue in Chapter 4, is Aquinas' great contribution to the natural law, what he offers that Aristotle never could. Reparation is a combination of pity and love. Though it is an over-simplification to reduce pity and love to caring for others (one reason it is an over-simplification is because we must also think responsibly about how we do so), surely reparation, pity, and love are related ideals.

There was not much talk about care among informants. Had the way of care been completely absent among informants, I might not have noticed, as the minimal social contract would have become the sea in which all fish, including the interviewer, swim. So I was surprised when Marc responded to my question about "the most important thing in the world" by saying, apropos of nothing that had come before (or perhaps I wasn't listening well that day), "I don't have to care for my neighbor like I do for my family. But I still have to care. If I can follow that one principle, then everything else is details."

What about some suffering soul in Africa, I replied after a longer than usual silence, someone you don't even know, whose way of life you can barely imagine?

"I still have to care . . . I just don't know how to put it into practice. Send money, I guess."

Marc was born and raised in a small town in Western Maryland, where his family has lived for generations. Two other informants who talked about care were raised in families still tied to the traditional culture of their foreign-born parents. Maya said that she is shocked at the carelessness and callousness of many Americans. Morality she says "means to behave in a manner in which one is not ashamed." She continues,

"When I walk down the street [of a big city near the university] I'm shocked at all the homeless people. It makes me feel less moral."

Do you mean it makes you feel ashamed, I asked?

"Yes, exactly. It makes me ashamed to be an American."

Maya says not one word about the social contract. Her context is care and shame. Then she goes on to say something truly shocking, for I had not heard its like before.

"Most humans aren't good. Not just Americans. I mean most people."

Taken aback, all I could think to ask was how this fit in with her morality.

To Maya the answer was obvious. "Because most people aren't good, they have to be taught to feel shame at the right things. People don't have to be good. They just have to be taught."

Should people feel shame for not caring, I asked.

"Absolutely, that's number one."

What did Maya mean by care? What did Marc mean? Did they mean what Carol Gilligan (1982) meant when she referred to the "care perspective" in *In a Different Voice?* Here I am not concerned with whether women do in fact reason differently from men, an issue raised by Gilligan that remains far from settled. I intend only to characterize the care perspective, in order to see if it describes the care that informants are talking about.

With the term "care," Gilligan refers to a way of experiencing the world that sees moral problems as marked by how we show concern for and responsibility to particular others, rather than as a problem of rights and rules. "Thus, the logic underlying an ethic of care is a psychological logic of relationships, which contrasts with the formal logic of fairness that informs the justice approach" (Gilligan 1982, 73). From the perspective of care, I need to gather all the information I can, all the details that are generally absent from hypothetical situations, in order to minimize the chances of hurting anyone. Against the care perspective Gilligan sets what is often called universal morality, the morality of Immanuel Kant (1991) for example, which determines our obligations by figuring out which general rules apply to a particular situation.

The short answer is that Gilligan's concept of care doesn't fit informants' use of the term. Though my sample is too small to be more than suggestive (Gilligan never discusses her sample size or characteristics), when the few informants who do talk about care do so, they talk in universalistic and abstract terms. In other words, they talk about care in terms that are oxymoronic as Gilligan formulates the concept. Certainly this could be an artifact of my research topic, natural law.

But, both Marc and Maya turn quickly to personal experiences – in particular, to personal struggles with how to care for anonymous others. Though I raised the issue with Marc, I did not push that particular reading of the natural law on either of them. Rather, they saw it as a particularly problematic, troublesome, pressing, and real moral problem, and it is hard for me to disagree with them.

What seems to be happening with Marc and Maya, as well as the two or three other informants who also talked in terms of care, is that the unstructured questions I asked turned them away from hypothetical scenarios such as "Should Heinz steal a drug he can't afford to buy in order to save his wife's life?" (a standard stage of moral development test question employed by Gilligan, as well as her teacher and *bête noire*, Lawrence Kohlberg), and toward real world ethical problems they face as thoughtful young men and women almost every day of their lives. Above all how to care for the suffering of those whom they barely know, or may never even see, except perhaps on television? In such circumstances, care itself becomes the problem. Not whether to care or to follow universal rules, but how to care in an anonymous, rationalized world in which human suffering seems endless, and often nameless and faceless as well.

Or as Jean put it, "I know how to care for my friends and my family. Oh, I don't usually get it right, but I have the basic idea. What I don't know how to do is care for the people who need it most, people who live in some country I've never heard of, people I'll never meet, never even see, except on television, and then I'll probably turn it off because I'm eating dinner. But I won't be able to turn it off in my head, if you know what I mean."

Here is a dimension of the problem of caring that does not even arise in Gilligan's account. Nor does it arise in George Steiner's account of that telluric place in which the "loving immediacy of unquestioning care" is "the rule of human relations." Indeed, Steiner, Gilligan, and Antigone come closer to each other than to my informants, who struggle with an even more difficult question: how to find a place for care in a political (indeed, global) world that has no place for such personal impulses, whose very size and anonymity seem to drive out the human connections upon which care is based? I don't know the answer to this question, but it seems to me that it is the more important and difficult question in our era.

Though this dimension of the problem of caring does not arise in Gilligan's account, it does appear in a surprising place: in the preamble to the United Nations Universal Declaration of Human Rights, which refers to "the equal and inalienable rights of all members of the human family" as "the foundation of freedom, justice, and peace in the world" (Glendon 2001, 310). The purpose of the preamble, according to its author, René Cassin, was to establish an intellectual or philosophical perspective from which to understand the rights enumerated by the Declaration. That perspective, it turns out, was remarkably similar to the care perspective. To be sure, diplomats generally don't use the language of the care perspective per se. My point is that the Declaration was conceived less as a liberal document, and more as an expression of

the dignitarian rights tradition of continental Europe and Latin America.... Dignitarian rights instruments, with their emphasis on the family, and their greater attention to duties, are more compatible with Asian and African tradition. In these documents, rights bearers tends to be envisioned within families and communities... (Glendon 2001, 227)

It is this dignitarian tradition that comes remarkably close to the care perspective. Not the care perspective of Gilligan, but that of several informants, who struggle with how to care for abstract and anonymous others.

One should perhaps not make too much of intellectual foundations of morality, particularly as far as the United Nations Declaration of Human Rights is concerned. Jacques Maritain, who played a leading role in the UNESCO philosophers' committee, which advised the Declaration drafting committee, liked to tell the story of how a visitor to one meeting was amazed that men of such vastly different cultures, beliefs, and ideologies could agree on a list of fundamental rights. Yes, the man was told, "we agree about the rights but on the condition no one asks us why" (Glendon 2001, 77).[5] The tougher question is

---

[5] The UNESCO philosophers' advisory group advised the Declaration drafting committee, chaired by Eleanor Roosevelt, and later Charles Malik. Maritain evidently did not regard the lack of agreement on foundations as fatal, understanding that the Declaration was a practical document, not a profession of faith (Glendon 2001, 77–78). The sadder part of the story is that the drafting committee apparently did not find the philosophers' work particularly helpful or relevant. Several felt UNESCO was treading on their turf, an old bureaucratic story (Glendon 2001, 83–84).

whether the experience of care, whatever it is called, must become attenuated unto nothingness as it is extended to encompass a family too big to be a real family – the human family. Can a species ever become a family? Or perhaps I am being too literal. Perhaps the care we receive in families remains a useful moral metaphor or narrative for those with the imagination to adopt it.

Absent Inwardness?

What seems to distinguish those few informants who care from the social contract theorists, especially the metaphysical biologists, is the quality of their inner worlds. Indeed, the absence of apparent inwardness among most informants is my most subtle and striking finding. By an absence of "inwardness" I mean difficulty thinking in the moral subjunctive.

When posed as an abstract ideal, the vast majority of informants understand the minimal natural law as something that is the case. Furthermore, most can give grounds that in themselves bridge (some might say ignore) the venerable is/ought distinction. Metaphysical biology was the leading bridge. The vast majority of informants can also understand the natural law as something that is either present or absent in the posited laws and practices of a particular regime, say Saudi Arabia, even if they do not use the language of "posit" and "positive law."

Far fewer informants can think in the moral subjunctive – that is, recognize that natural law might exist, even when it is notably and demonstrably absent. In other words, far fewer informants possess the capacity of Antigone. To be sure, it is a subtle and complicated story, for most informants are not troubled by the absent presence of the natural law if it is not dramatically pointed out to them. For example, not everyone in the United States is secure in life, liberty, and person. Once absent presence becomes problematic, however, a surprising number of informants became confused, as they tend to think of "existence" as a binary category: either natural law is present or absent.

About this conclusion I am not as confident as I would like to be, as none of my questions were specifically designed to address the problem. It is an issue that came up in conversation with almost a dozen informants. Consider Joseph, who quickly and emphatically agreed with Article 3 of the UN Declaration, which states "Everyone has a right to life, liberty, and security of person."

Instead of asking Joseph what he would say to someone who disagreed, I asked him (for no particular reason I can think of) what he would say about the life of women in Saudi Arabia?

Suddenly Joseph become confused, even agitated. Was it the topic of women, Saudi Arabia? As he went on, I realized his problem was that I had created for him what was an impossible category: something that existed that was not supposed to exist.

"I don't understand," said Joseph. "It really doesn't make any sense to me. How can universal rights exist if they don't exist somewhere? I think I must have been mistaken in my answer. How can everyone have a right to something that doesn't exist everywhere? It just doesn't make sense, either everyone has it or no one does."

Does that mean that because women in Saudi Arabia lack basic human rights, then human rights don't exist.

"Yes," said Joseph. "I'd say that's true." With that he folded his arms, looked at the space between our feet, and that was that.

Contrast Joseph with Larry, whom I interviewed shortly after Joseph, and with whom I used the same Saudi example. "Sure, these women in Saudi Arabia have the same universal rights as you and me, but that doesn't really mean anything. To make rights real you have to fight for them. No one is going to give them to you."

Ernst Bloch, the Marxist theologian, makes a similar claim in *Natural Law and Human Dignity*. "Genuine natural law, which posits the free will in accord with reason, was the first to reclaim the justice that can only be obtained by struggle" (Bloch 1986, xxx).

Bloch and Larry both recognize that something may be real, but nonetheless may never be realized except through struggle, a struggle that is not guaranteed to succeed. Many informants could not match their subtlety. If basic human rights are protected and practiced, then they exist. If these rights are not protected and practiced, then they don't exist, at least not for those unlucky enough to live under a repressive regime. (There is a cliché to the effect that no one is free until everyone is free. As piece of inspirational political poetry it has its place. As an account of how to think about the natural law it is not very helpful.)

Doesn't my argument about Joseph and his compatriots contradict my earlier claim that most informants are metaphysical biologists, and that the vast majority adhere to the minimal natural law? No. Here I'm talking about something more subtle: not informants' adherence to the minimal natural law, but the quality of the moral imagination behind their analysis of the presence or absence of the natural law at work in the world.

How many compatriots did Joseph have? I cannot say for sure, as I did not employ the "counterfactual strategy" with every informant. When I did, more informants became more confused and disoriented than I would have imagined: over half of the dozen or so I challenged in this way. Had I challenged every informant as I did Joseph, I do not believe this ratio would have held up. Many informants were just too imaginative to be flummoxed by this question. I do, however, believe I would have discovered still more informants disoriented and confused by the moral subjunctive.

In claiming that many informants cannot think in the moral subjunctive, am I not violating my own injunction not to assume that informants are acting on motives they deny? No. This is not a straightforward topic about which I could ask "Are you capable of thinking about natural law in the moral subjunctive?" Rather, I had to ask questions the implications of which were subtle and indirect, listen carefully, and draw my own conclusions. About what to make of these conclusions I am not sure, so I have turned to Herbert Marcuse for assistance.

Marcuse (1970) would likely argue that informants suffer from what he called the "massification of domination," by which he meant the disappearance of any inner space of resistance, the result of not having to fight for one's freedom. What Jean-Paul Sartre (1956) calls *Néant* is similar to this inner space, an arena of psychic negation in which one can affirm or deny the existence of anything. Is there, I wondered, a connection between the limited idealizing imagination of many informants, which I judge to be unfortunate, and their refusal to be troubled by the naturalistic fallacy, expressed most keenly by the metaphysical biologists, who see empirical equality ("we all come from the same place") not simply as implying moral equality, but as being virtually the same thing. This I judge *not* to be unfortunate. At its worst, natural law may become that garland of transcendental flowers that covers our earthly chains. For all their limits, the metaphysical biologists among informants are unlikely to succumb to this particular ideology.

It was during my encounter with the metaphysical biology of the majority of informants that I became aware that they were not thinking about natural law like I was thinking about natural law. At first I thought they were, that they were arguing in an almost traditional natural law fashion, interpreting nature under the principle of reason, albeit a radically simplified reason, more concerned with existence than the pursuit of the good. In the end metaphysical biology is too literal to support any but the simplest expression of the good, such as Article 3 of the United Nations Declaration of Human Rights. If one cannot think in the moral subjunctive – if one has difficulty imagining a right that does not exist in the real world, but only in the world of the moral imagination – then natural law will be of limited value.

Limited value is not the same as no value. The world would be a better place if every regime respected just this one article. My point is more abstract. Metaphysical biology is the opposite of teleological thinking, which sees the present in terms of its potential. Metaphysical biology sees the present in terms of the present. The concept of "potential" is absent, which is of course why teleological thinking is missing from informants' accounts. Metaphysical biology is lowest common denominator morality. The self-evident social contract is only a little more sophisticated, recognizing basic relationships as goods in themselves, but nonetheless holding to a minimal view of what these basic relationships morally entail.

A question I can raise, but not answer, is the degree to which the impoverishment of informants' inner worlds is related to the loss of a richer narrative tradition. To be sure, there is no requirement that the natural law be expressed in religious terms. On the contrary, the new natural law theorists are not the first to use the natural law as a way of appealing to what all men and women have in common regardless of their religious beliefs (or nonbeliefs). Nevertheless, the Judeo-Christian tradition fills in the plot outline of the minimal natural law with a rich, darkly luminous narrative whose beauty and terror has never been equaled in the West. Almost all who write in a profound and significant vein about the meaning of life (for that is truly our topic), such as Melanie Klein, write in the shadow of this tradition.

Edward Glover was not being overly dramatic when he called Klein a theorist of Original Sin (Rudnytsky 1994, 46).

Nevertheless, I agree with Marcuse (1978) that more than one literary genre may foster a rich inner world. Consider the high bourgeois novel, with its promise of happiness (*promesse de bonheur*) forever unfulfilled. It too may foster a deep, if tortured, inner world, characterized by a vital space between reality and fantasy. As an example of this tradition, Marcuse cites Flaubert's *Madam Bovary*. One might respond that Emma Bovary is hardly an exemplary character. True enough; indeed, that is precisely the point. In her spare world, anyone who wants more than the conventional portion of happiness allotted her is at risk of destroying herself from within through envy and greed. It is by allowing characters like Emma to enter our souls that we are inspired to create new possibilities for good and evil. Above all, we develop an imagination able to think in terms of "not now but someday, not now but maybe." Maybe there could be a world in which Emma would not have to destroy herself and her family in order to have a chance at happiness. Of course, most – indeed virtually all – high bourgeois art, including *Madam Bovary*, is an encounter with the Judeo-Christian tradition. It would be a mistake to separate the high bourgeois novel from the Judeo-Christian tradition. To struggle, even to reject this tradition, is still to be enriched by it. James Joyce's *A Portrait of the Artist as a Young Man* is a classic example.[6]

While I don't know the degree to which impoverished inner worlds reflect grossly simplified narrative regimes, it is striking that MacIntyre's (1981) account of the (post) modern condition fits hardly a single informant. Informants were not lost and incoherent in their views. Nor did they use ethical terms in ways that had long lost any connection to moral reality. Instead, informants live in coherent but

---

[6] The finest, simplest, and most straightforward account of the risks of reading appeared in the *The New York Times*. In it, Edmundson (2004) brings Marcuse down to twenty-first century earth.

Yet for many people, the process of socialization doesn't quite work. The values they acquire from all the well-meaning authorities don't fit them. And it is these people who often become obsessed readers. They don't read for information, and they don't read for beautiful escape. No, they read to remake themselves. They read to be socialized again, not into the ways of their city or village this time but into another world with different values. . . . They want to adopt values they perceive to be higher or perhaps just better suited to their natures.

abridged moral worlds. This may not be a great deal better, but one cannot cure the disorder until one gets the diagnosis right. Furthermore, the nature of the disorder is not as straightforward as first appears. What looks like an abridged moral world is perhaps more accurately described as an intensely private one. The term "moral isolation" might be more accurate, as informants were generally unable to use a public language to explain their moral sentiments, which were, I often felt, less abridged than the words they drew upon to describe them. Robert Bellah (1985) and his associates make this argument at length in *Habits of the Heart*, a phrase they take from Alexis de Tocqueville. Many Americans long to give of themselves to their communities, but lack any language that would make sense of this desire even to themselves.

Something similar is happening with Americans' desire to be good. An old religious language is no longer convincing to many, and nothing has taken its place. While some cultural critics argue that this has led to "relativism," the first thing to say about this charge is that relativism is a more complex phenomenon, with a longer and more complex history, than many who use the term seem prepared to admit. Or rather, the term is often used as though it were a curse, capable of paralyzing an opponent just by uttering it. In fact, some versions of relativism, particularly Protagorean relativism, are not distant from the natural law. Let us parse the term before moving on.

Relativisms and The Natural Law

"Cultural relativism" is a fact of life. Different cultures do in fact disagree over basic values, though we must be careful not to exaggerate. Do different societies disagree over the fact that murder is wrong, or do they define murder differently?

"Normative relativism" goes on to equate the empirical fact of actual disagreement with the philosophical assertion that this is all there is. There exist no grounds to say anything more: good and bad, right and wrong, depend entirely upon the cultural definitions of these terms, as there is nothing higher or more fundamental.

There is, however, an intermediate position called "metaethical relativism." Denying ethical objectivism (there is always just one correct moral evaluation), metaethical relativism does not hold that all moral evaluations are equally worthy. One may believe that there is more than one morally worthy solution, more than one account of the good life, and yet not believe that all are equally good. There are stopping places on the slippery slope from moral objectivism to normative relativism.

Nobody thinks that there are necessary and sufficient conditions which will pick out, for example, the unique referent of the 'best thing for her to have done on finding herself in that rather embarrassing situation,' though plausible conditions can be given which will shorten a list of competing incompatible candidates. Why should it be different for the referents of what she should have done in that ghastly moral dilemma or 'the Good Life for man.' (Rorty 1979, 373–374)

Because there is more than one morally worthy solution does not mean there are an infinite number, or that anything goes. Imagine that the "rather embarrassing situation" was to have broken an expensive vase while attending a cocktail party given by a wealthy friend. What she should have done depends on how well off the vase breaker is, whether she broke it while drunk and disorderly, how close her friendship with the owner was, and so forth. But one can imagine lots of things she should *not* have done under any circumstances: laugh it off, break another vase, pretend it didn't happen, blame it on someone else, and so forth. The analogy isn't perfect, even if morals and manners share a common French root, *mores*. But the idea makes sense: that there is not one good way of life, one human telos, does not mean that one way of life is as good as another, that any telos goes.

It is in this vein that there is a connection between Protagorean relativism and the vision of natural law that I (and even Veatch) promote. If, that is, one holds, as many scholars do, that the "man" in "man is the measure of all things" refers to humanity in general, not a particular individual. For then we are talking about what best suits human beings, given their nature as humans. Seen from this perspective, Protagoras is doctor to humanity, saying simply that humanity is the measure of what works to cure humans of their illnesses, their failure to thrive. As with most illnesses, there may be more than one medicine that works, but there are even more that don't, and quite a few that are poisonous.

These distinctions are for the chapters that follow. For now the problem is not primarily moral relativism, but moral minimalism. Moral minimalism is attractive in its inventiveness, as well as its adherence to the core of the natural law. But moral minimalism is deeply disturbing in its lack of moral imagination, as well as in the way it may serve as an excuse for not taking the morality of everyday life seriously, a life in which we are generally not asked to kill innocents (at least not personally; we may be asked as citizens to consent to their murder), but may find it advantageous to lie to fellow citizens. About this, the minimal natural law has little to say, and few stories to fall back on.

It may be that moral minimalism is a worse problem than Protagorean relativism. Certainly this possibility cannot be dismissed in advance, even as I do not believe this is the proper formulation of the issue. For now the key point is that we should not confuse minimalism and relativism. The question I cannot answer is whether this confusion among many intellectuals is in the end empirical, or ideological. Have these intellectuals really not noticed the difference? Or have they not wished to notice the difference, as relativism is the more convenient and popular term of abuse?

CONCLUSION

The moral relativist to whom so many refer, and against whom so many are rendered speechless, seems not to exist, at least not among those whom one most expects to find him or her, the young. To put it more precisely, relativism is absent among the young whom I interviewed, most of whom hold to a minimal version of the natural law. Conversely, cultural critics such as MacIntyre and Bloom write as though the secular relativist dominates the culture. In fact, the ethics committee on which I served was fighting a phantom. Not moral relativism, but moral minimalism, is the problem.

This may not seem like an important distinction, but I believe it is. Academics devote an enormous amount of time to grounding or founding moral claims, or (more commonly these days) showing why that is impossible, indeed undesirable, an act of intellectual imperialism. Jean-François Lyotard famously defines postmodernity as incredulity toward metanarratives (Lyotard 1984, xxiv). Yet it is upon a metanarrative that informants base their morality – a minimalist metanarrative to be sure, but it is still a metanarrative, not a mininarrative.

Theirs is not a mininarrative because while it lacks character, detail, and development, all the things we look for in a good story, Article 3 of the United Nations Declaration and its like are nonetheless about the most important things. There is nothing mini about life, liberty, and security of person. Nor is there anything mini about the universality of the social contract, even if many informants have trouble with its subjunctive version. Thus, it is incorrect to state, as did a well-known and respected theorist of the natural law who responded to a version of this chapter when presented at a conference, that informants have abandoned the hierarchy of goods traditionally associated with the natural law. No, they have simply truncated the hierarchy, so that it stops short.

The difference between abandoning and truncating the hierarchy is important in determining if the minimal natural law provides more to work with than the liberalism that is supposedly everywhere triumphant. There is, after all, a difference between seeing human freedom as the highest value because it allows individuals to choose, and a viewpoint which sees the equality of all humans under the (admittedly truncated) natural law as the highest value. Under the former perspective, the choosing individual is rendered sacred; under the later, it is the metaphysical bond among individuals, what they share, that is, if not sacred, then at least the locus of value. Or as Veatch (2005) puts it, do we believe in natural rights because people have rights merely by virtue of being individuals, or because we believe that it is right that all people observe the natural rights of others? Informants come a bit closer to the second sense of natural right than the first. That's actually a big difference, and a big deal. Enough so that I shall have to revise my statement that only several informants share the care perspective. Only several informants articulate the care perspective; it is latent but implicit in the worldviews of more.

Why do I say this? Because metaphysical biology (and here I include "the social contract as a basic good in itself" as a version of metaphysical biology, though metaphysical sociology would be a more accurate term) is about what humans possess in common. For all that it lacks in teleological ambition, metaphysical biology possesses a keen sense of humans as common creatures, in the double sense of sharing much, as well as being at heart ordinary and unrefined. This perspective on humanity should be neither underestimated nor undervalued, particularly by those who aspire to the higher reaches of the natural law. Though no one put it as Freud did ("we are born between urine and faeces"), I don't believe it was an accident that this phrase kept recurring to me as I listened to informants describe what we have in common.

We all come from the same place, and we are headed for the same grave. There's nothing all that special about you, or about me. We are just naked biological beings in this world together for a little while, so we had better not put on airs, and not pretend that anyone is better than anyone else.

No informant put it quite this way, but this is the implication of metaphysical biology for most as far as the natural law is concerned.

Such a view, by the way, is quite compatible with considerable income inequality, as long as it does not threaten life, liberty, or security of person. In economics, hard work and luck play leading roles, and Raymond's (the would-be note stealer) reasoning tends to prevail. People are enough alike that right now they are figuring out how to climb over me, so I had better get to work figuring out how to climb over them. Needed are basic rules, not the welfare state.[7]

The result is hardly an image of man or woman *imago Dei*. Nor is the result one that aspires to hierarchies of virtue, development, or goodness. One would hope for something more elevated. And yet let us not overlook what is here to work with: an abstract (because it is based on an idea) but body based and hence real, not ideal, sense of commonality (but not community) among all persons. What we have in common comes first. Here is the nonliberal, nonindividualistic basis of the minimum natural law. At least this is the implication of metaphysical biology. The implication is not elevated, but it has little to do with the liberalism, or relativism, or most of the other "isms" that critics of the culture seem to find there.

And yet a puzzle remains. If informants hold a nonliberal justification of the natural law, it is hardly in the "dignitarian" tradition to which Glendon refers, and not just because it does not sound very "dignified." In responding to critics of the United Nations Declaration of Human Rights who argued that it reflected Western values, the Declarations' drafters, as well as the UNESCO philosophers who advised

---

[7] Readers interested in learning more about young people's thinking about economic inequality can read my *Rethinking Freedom* (Alford 2005). It is based on interviews about money, power, and freedom with a group of young people demographically comparable to those interviewed in this chapter.

them, repeatedly invoked the similarity among all human beings. "Their starting point was the simple fact of the common humanity shared by every man, woman and child on the earth, a fact that, for them, put linguistic, racial, religious and other differences into their proper perspective." All, continues Glendon (2001, 232–233), would have agreed with a statement made by a representative of Human Rights Watch/Asia in 1993. "Whatever else may separate them, human beings belong to a single biological species, the simplest and most fundamental commonality before which the significance of human differences quickly fades."

Put aside, dear reader, for just a moment your philosophies of *différeance*, whether you spell the term in English or French. Put aside for a moment whether you think Glendon et al. are denying real human differences, and ask yourself the following question: why is it that the simple fact of shared humanity, including the recognition that we are a single species, leads the drafters of the UN Declaration to a complex and elaborate account of what we owe each other, whereas the simple fact of shared biological humanity leads my informants to a limited, truncated view of what we owe each other? This, I believe, is the puzzle we have only begun to solve. The answer, I believe, has to do with the biological reductionism of informants. Informants mean something different by shared humanity. Not entirely different, of course, but shared humanity means something more literal, less imaginative. With Marcuse I have speculated about the sources of the literal and less imaginative quality of some informants' thinking, and I will continue to do so along the way.

For now it seems best to conclude with an example of how *not* to teach and argue about our mutual obligations. The example is found in T. M. Scanlon's (1998) *What We Owe Each Other*. Lest the reader think I am picking on an author, let me assure the reader that Scanlon's is one of the finest works of its kind in recent decades. Neither the author nor the book, but the intellectual species, is my target.

Why is it wrong to throw hazardous radioactive debris out of my airplane on the people below if I will never meet them, and never need to land there? And why would I do this? Perhaps because it makes the sunset more beautiful. The answer to the act's wrongness, Scanlon believes, must be found in the airborne litterer's inability to justify this act to others in rational discourse. Scanlon is, in other words, searching for nonmoral grounds for morality, as so many academics do (McGinn 1999).[8] The academic obsession with founding and grounding on the one hand, deconstruction and the hermeneutics of suspicion on the other, addresses an audience composed, at most, of several thousand other academics.

How much better to begin with the moral intuitions of most people (an approach famously practiced by Aristotle), which turns out to be, at least for the young people I spoke with, a minimalist version of natural law. Build on this basis, criticize it, all while taking the moral intuitions of citizens seriously. It was the inability of the members of the ethics committee, to whom I referred at the beginning of this chapter, to take their own moral intuitions seriously that paralyzed them. Academics could be helpful here, but only if they make an effort to learn and speak the moral language of everyday life. Ironically enough, that turns out to be a version of the natural law. One reason it is ironic is because it is a version compatible with most of the venial sins. Another reason it is ironic is that many academics cannot get even this far, getting stuck at questions such as why we shouldn't drop uranium on people from airplanes if it happens to make the sunset more radiant.

Academics did not create this world of moral abstraction. Credit belongs to the modern world itself, best summarized by what Max Weber called the iron cage of rationalization, in which it seems every aspect of one's life, including one's soul, comes to be managed by bureaucrats and experts (Weber 1958, 181). Important is that academics not further this process, rendering citizens even more defenseless when asked to explain their moral intuitions. Instead, academics should help clarify, develop, and expand these intuitions. The language of natural law, which joins intuition with tradition, community, and shared narrative, provides a moral lingua franca that comes closer to how average people think than many academics (including myself at the beginning of my research) recognize. But first we have to learn what moral intuitions people actually hold, and what there is to work

[8] McGinn (1999) attributes this particular example to Scanlon; I think it is McGinn's. Though the distinction is of no theoretical import, as far as I can tell Scanlon (1998, 168) writes about sending hazardous waste to places we will never visit, and about throwing debris out of my airplane as I fly over places where I will never land. I do not believe Scanlon combines the two examples as McGinn evidently does.

with. That was the purpose of the research on which this chapter is based.

The conclusion of Chapter 4 returns to the young people interviewed here, asking whether the minimal natural law is an undeveloped version of the real (or reparative) natural law, or is the minimal natural law a dead end? Otherwise expressed, is the minimal natural law merely a version of H. L. A. Hart's positivistic natural law, which like Hobbes's natural law remains destined to develop no further? Or is the potential of the minimal natural law greater, more akin to a question waiting for an answer? I think the minimal natural law is closer to the latter, an impulse to reparation in a world bereft not only of the language of reparation, but of the social and cultural containment that could make reparation moral.

APPENDIX

The following questions were asked of twenty-four informants. The remaining six answered a shorter questionnaire composed of questions 1, 2, 3, 6, 8, and 10. Almost every response elicited by the longer questionnaire was elicited by the shorter, while providing a somewhat more relaxed atmosphere for discussion.

1. The UN Declaration of Human Rights says that "Everyone has a right to life, liberty and security of person" [Article 3]. Do you think this is true? How would you answer someone who said "That's ridiculous!"?

2. You're in a tough chemistry class in which it seems that almost everyone cheats. The professor doesn't seem to care, leaving the classroom during exams for long periods of time. On the midterm you got a D. The people who cheated got all As and Bs. It's time to take the final. What do you do? Why?

3. You're on a committee developing the new moral education curriculum at Thomas Jefferson High School. What's the single most important thing you should teach? What if someone disagrees, saying that in some cultures it's considered OK to [content based on response to A]. What do you say?

4. The UN Declaration of Human Rights says "All human beings are born free and equal in dignity and rights" [Article 1]. Do you

think it's true? What if someone says "No, I think some people are better than others and ought to have more rights." What do you say?

5. You are working on a government contract. Your company is in economic trouble, and your boss asks you to over bill the government – that is, bill the government for hours that you didn't work. If you don't, the company might go under, and many would lose their jobs. What would you do? Why?

6. What's the most important thing in the world? Why?

7. Imagine that you are about fifty years old. As a young man/woman, you were very aggressive in getting to the top. Along the way you told some lies, and ruined some reputations. Some people were hurt. Now you regret that deeply. What do you do about it?

8. What is morality? Why be moral?

9. What if someone said to you "I lie, cheat, and steal anytime I think I can get away with it. Sometimes I get caught, but it's worth it. I do it for the thrill, like playing the lottery." What do you say or do? What do you think?

10. What's the worst thing in the world? Why?

Most interviews took place in my office, which is fairly comfortable, with pictures of my grandchildren around. Generally I offered the informant tea or coffee. In other words, I attempted to offset the persistent questioning ("Why do you think that way?" "That doesn't quite make sense to me.") with a humane environment and attitude. It seemed to work. A number of interviews took place in informants' homes.

My research was approved by the Human Subjects Review Committee of my university.

3

Natural Law and Natural Evil

Recall that it is the paradigmatic natural law theorist, Thomas Aquinas, who defines the prime principle of natural law as do good, avoid evil (ST I–II 94, 2). For some of the new natural law theorists, as they are called, such as Finnis (1980), and George (1999), the statement is strictly analytic, true by virtue of the way we use the terms good and evil. From the perspective of Melanie Klein, the prime principle of natural law is filled with empirical content. Do good, avoid evil assumes that that one has always already wanted to destroy the good because it is good, beyond me and my control, because the good is not me or mine. Knowing one's evil means knowing something of the power of the death drive within oneself, one's lust to destroy the good. That too is part of the history of that telluric place where Steiner finds Antigone's inspiration. It is the same place where Milton's Satan resides in *Paradise Lost,* the place whose motto reads "Evil be thou my Good" (IV, 105–110).

In an important respect I agree with Russell Hittinger (2003), who argues that talk about natural law is today both abundant and degraded. Once natural law comes to be seen as an "instrument of persuasion," its truth comes to be measured by its success in achieving consensus. Soon this consensus *is* natural law, a conclusion Hittinger would apply to the new natural law theorists, such as Finnis and George, for they construct their list of basic goods from what people say they want.

An encouraging aspect of my interviews with young people is that while their understanding of the natural law is minimal, it is not degraded, for they do not see themselves as involved in acts of persuasion or performance. On the contrary, the minimal natural law, for all its limits and defects, resides within the great tradition of the natural law, binding nature with moral obligation. This is so even as the natural hierarchy is truncated. Reparative natural law resides within the same great tradition, continuing to bind nature with moral obligation. This is so even as the nature in question is human, and Hume must continue to have his say. Even if human nature is constructed roughly along the lines described by Aristotle and Aquinas, there exist no grounds to conclude that we "ought" to live according to this nature. Nature is discovered; ought is created by the decision to observe certain values. Between these two realms there is a chasm, one that a belief in God can no longer bridge, as we live in a secular world.

In response to this criticism the new natural law was born. People still talk and act as if goods such as life, friendship, health, knowledge, beauty, and play are good in themselves. For example, we desire money in order to acquire things (that is, money is an instrumental good), but health is a good in itself. Goods in themselves do not require further justification, and because they are *already* values, one is not committing the naturalistic fallacy in saying we ought to pursue them. Furthermore, because these goods are not themselves moral values, but premoral, or so Finnis and George argue, the freedom of the individual is preserved. Not enmeshed and obligated moral beings, but free agents who would naturally (selfishly) choose these goods for themselves, are the subjects of the new natural law (George 1999, 45).

The problem with the empirical approach to natural law (the approach is "empirical" because it takes what is said to be desirable as truly desirable) is not only is there no hierarchy among goods, but no developmental ideal remains. Abandoned is the principle that some goods are more important and profound than others. No longer part of a big story, the new natural law seems ideally suited for a contemporary world that no longer believes in metanarratives.

In the absence of a "speculative philosophy of nature" by which to order the hierarchy among goods, Germain Grisez (1965) and Finnis (1980) posit what they call "modes of responsibility," to guide us in choosing among goods. Otherwise, I might choose to continue chatting with friends instead of preventing a child playing nearby from running into traffic. (If basic goods are equally valuable, who is to say that a child's life is more important than pursuing the pleasures of friendship?) In developing "modes of responsibility," the new natural law theorists believe they have met the objection that they can neither find nor posit a hierarchy among goods.

Modes of responsibility are, in fact, familiar moral guidelines, even if they do not always look so familiar when expressed in academic-speak, such as "choose and otherwise will those and only those possibilities whose willing is compatible with integral human fulfillment" (George 1999, 51). A more familiar way of expressing the leading principle is in terms of Kantian universalism. "A person," wrote Immanuel Kant, "is subject to no other laws than those which he (either alone or jointly with others) gives to himself" (Kant 1991, 50). Because I would want someone else to break off a conversation with friends to save my child, then I must will that moral hierarchy for myself as well as others. One can readily see why several critics of the new natural law see it as Kantianism in disguise. Indeed, as Veatch (2005) has argued, that seems to have been the fate of the natural law for many years now.

Another way of putting this same point is that ever since Kant, scholars have been practicing "as if" natural law. Like the Kantian categorical imperative, moral principles are issued as if they were principles of the natural law, but upon closer inspection one quickly realizes that nature itself is treated as valueless: external to reason, and hence of no moral consequence. This is certainly the position of the new natural law theorists. The devaluation or epistemological disappearance of nature arises, one suspects, not merely from an overscrupulous observance of the is/ought distinction, but from a way of thinking that remains committed to interpreting human progress in terms of humanity's liberation from nature. Ironic is how a position so essential to the Enlightenment has become essential to postmodernism as well, which argues that there is no path from text to world. We are trapped in text, from which there is no exit (Kainz 2004, 41–42, 73; Devine 2000, 55).

Is it possible, I will be asking with the help of Klein, to see human excellence in teleological terms that participate in nature, even if the nature in question begins and ends with human beings? Or perhaps even Klein would involve the cosmos, much as Freud invokes the battle between Eros and Thanatos for the life of the human species. With Freud, I invoke the language of narrative and metaphor, but it is MacIntyre (1981) who has taught us that narrative is the teleology of the modern world. In other words, narrative may take the place of ancient and medieval teleology.

Every human life itself has a narrative structure (even if for most young people this narrative is impoverished), for story is the way humans naturally give meaning to our lives. Or as Barbara Hardy puts it, "we dream in narrative, daydream in narrative, remember, anticipate, hope, despair, believe, doubt, plan, revise, criticize, construct, gossip, learn, hate and love by narrative" (Hardy 1968, 5). Furthermore, as narratology, the study of narrative, has taught us, stories are defined by their end. Everything that happens before is reinterpreted in light of how it all turns out in the end. Without an ending there can be no plot, and hence no satisfactory meaning (Prince 1987, 26). Narrative is the teleology of everyday life. Narratives about human nature are neither self-contradictory (the claim that they are really all narrative, and no nature) nor self-referential (the claim that they never escape the web of narrative). Or rather, narratives about human nature are no more self-referential than narratives about anything else in the world.

Pamela Hall (1994, 94) has turned the narrative approach to Thomas in *Narrative and the Natural Law: An Interpretation of Thomistic Ethics*, arguing that "we learn the natural law, not by deduction, but by reflection upon our own and our predecessors' desires, choices, mistakes, and successes." This reflection is, in large measure, conducted with others – that is, as dialogue. It is this aspect of Aquinas that Maritain captures so brilliantly, including (unfortunately) an unwarranted confidence in historical progress. It is, in any case, no longer possible to argue convincingly that Thomas belongs to the schoolmen. Thomas belongs to all who value a meaningful story about the good life.

A LITTLE BIT OF KLEIN

What I call reparative natural law is inspired by the work of the psychoanalyst Melanie Klein, and so it will be useful to briefly survey aspects of her work. I promise to be brief and nontechnical. Earlier I said her themes were those of the Judeo-Christian tradition. For now I shall make a simpler claim – that her themes are those of all great literature – love, hate, death, and reparation. There is, of course, no contradiction between these two claims, only different levels of analysis.

Though Melanie Klein never thought of herself as a natural law theorist, others have come close to this conclusion, even if they do not use the language of natural law. Exemplary is Michael Rustin's (1991) appreciative account of Klein and the Kleinians as theorists of social justice in his *The Good Society and the Inner World.*

"Melanie Klein's investigation of the mental states of infancy gave rise to an intensely *social* view of the origins of the self." The pleasure in being fed is less important than being held and cared for, or rather these pleasures are inseparable. Contra Freud, pleasure is not the infant's goal. Pleasure is a mere "signpost to the object," the human relationship. Even the infant is social.

There are, by the way, affinities between Klein's view of the infant and that of Augustine, though one should not make too much of the similarities. "He could not yet speak and pale with jealousy and bitterness, glared at his brother sharing his mother's milk," says Augustine of a jealous baby (*Confessions* 1.vii.10). While the grown-up baby (aren't we all?) may one day feel guilt, there is no sense in Augustine of the love that from the beginning of life will contend with hate. There is no sense, in other words, of the love that leads to guilt, unless perhaps it is the love of God, and that comes later.

Rustin continues, "a second characteristic of Kleinian analysis was its emphasis on the ethical. Kleinian theory makes the development of moral capacities in the infant a criterion of normal personality development. Moral feelings are held to be innate, arising from the primary intensity of feelings of love and hate for the object."[1] From almost the beginning of life, and certainly by the age of six months, the infant feels not just satisfaction from being fed and cuddled, but gratitude, as well as hate and rage when these satisfactions are not forthcoming.

The third aspect of Kleinian thought has already been mentioned, "its teleological dimension. There is inherent in Kleinian theory the idea of a 'normal' pathway of development . . . The 'depressive

---

[1] One reason Kleinians refer to other people as "objects" is out of deference to Freudian drive theory, which refers to the object of a drive. Kleinians keep the term but in effect reject the theory. The other reason Kleinians use the term "object" is to suggest how long it takes to learn to see others as whole persons. Furthermore, almost every adult will from time to time relate to others as part objects. For many of us, "object" remains an ugly term by which to refer to people. Object relations theory, which Klein founded, could today better be called relations theory.

position' defined as a state of affairs that was normative . . . was held in some way to correspond to the potential of human nature."

With the term "depressive position," Klein refers to a developmental achievement in which one knows that one loves and hates the same person. Klein calls it "depressive" because she believes that the knowledge of how much we hate what we love, as well as how much hate there is in the world, must sadden any person, even a child, though both children and adults are often unaware that it is this that makes them sad (Klein, 1975d).

Against the depressive position, Klein posits the paranoid-schizoid position, which sounds sicker than it is. Klein calls this earliest organization of the defenses the paranoid-schizoid position in order to stress both the way in which the young child's fears take the form of phantasies of persecution, as well as the way in which he or she defends against persecution by splitting, a schizoid phenomenon, in which he or she does not let him or herself know what he or she knows.[2] Klein believes that the paranoid-schizoid position begins almost at birth. It is a normally occurring psychotic state, a formulation for which Klein was often criticized.

With the paranoid-schizoid position, Klein asserts that the alternative to acknowledging one's sadness at all the hatred and pain in the world, including that tiny amount (when measured against the hatred and pain of the planet) inflicted by oneself, is to divide the world into good and bad, locating the source of hatred and pain in the external bad object, as she calls it. "If I suffer, then someone bad must be causing it, then I must be under attack," would be an example of this way of thinking (Klein 1975a). The goal of normal human development is to enter into and remain within the depressive position, even if no human being is ever secure there. Klein calls them "positions" rather than "stages" to emphasize that the achievement of the depressive position is always unstable and subject to reversion.

Rustin continues, "one central theme of Kleinian theory, however, was . . . difficult to assimilate into its social thought. This was the emphasis on destructiveness and aggression – the concept of an innate 'death

---

[2] Kleinians always spell phantasy with a "ph," in order to distinguish it from daydreaming. For Klein, phantasy is the core content of the dynamic unconscious.

instinct' " (Rustin 1991, 147–149). For Klein, as for Freud, the conflict between love and hate is primary.

For Klein, hate is most frequently encountered as a paranoid fear of aggression, which she sees as one's own hatred projected into the world. The key problem of mental life for Klein is to separate one's love and hate sufficiently in early life to be able to integrate them later on. Otherwise we shall be forever confused as to what is good and what is bad, and so likely to confuse love and hate our whole lives long. For Klein, there is no deeper and more terrifying confusion than this, for it puts everything we love and care about at risk of being mistakenly destroyed by our own hate.

In ideal-typical development this need not happen. As the individual matures, the destructive elements of the self are split off and regained, over and over, until greater integration comes about.

As a result, the feeling of responsibility becomes stronger, and guilt and depression are more fully experienced. When this happens, the ego is strengthened, omnipotence of destructive impulses is diminished, together with envy, and the capacity for love and gratitude, stifled in the course of the splitting processes, is released. (Klein 1975c, 225)

This is the telos of normal development, and it is dependent on the integration of destructive, hateful, sadistic, and envious aspects of the self.

Rustin's account of Klein as a theorist of social justice in the tradition of Aristotle and the British socialists (quite a combination) makes it easier to argue that Klein is a natural law theorist. But in what sense? The link between psychoanalysis and the natural law has been developed most thoroughly between John Bowlby's attachment theory, developed out of his experiences with children removed from their parents during the Second World War, and evolutionary natural law theory. Larry Arnhart (1998, 109–110) makes much of Bowlby to support his argument in *Darwinian Natural Right*, a topic taken up in Chapter 4. Here it must suffice to state that Klein dives in deeper waters. Beneath these waters contend Eros and Thanatos, which are constantly being confused, which is why I began with *Antigone*. Heroine of the natural law, she draws her powers from a source too close to Thanatos for the rest of us to admire unabashedly or copy. Most importantly, we should know that this is so. Aspects of the traditional natural law, less so in

Aquinas than in Augustine, come closest to appreciating her danger-ous passage.

While both Freud and Klein set Eros against Thanatos, life against death, for Klein there is no Nirvana principle, no connection between the hatred and aggression of Thanatos and the peace and absence of stimulation that Freud writes of in *Beyond the Pleasure Principle* (1920, 34–43). For Freud, the *Todestrieb* ultimately seeks to return to the origin of things, a state of oblivion. There is, in other words, a type of satis-faction inherent in the *Todestrieb*, a satisfaction from which life itself is a long detour. For Klein, on the other hand, the *Todestrieb* is sadism, envy, and destruction. Nothing in Klein's account of the *Todestrieb* sug-gests she shared Freud's idea that death is the telos of life (Alford 1989, 25).

This might make it seem as if Klein's account of the "death instinct" would be easier to assimilate into mainstream psychoanalytic thought that Freud's. That may not be the case, for Klein makes it clear that the infant and young child hates, envies, and would destroy its mother if it could, regardless of how responsive and loving mother truly is. To be sure, Klein and Kleinians recognize that the mother's response to the child's aggression, how well she is able to contain the child's hatred and envy, will make an enormous difference in how well the child is able to integrate its experiences of loving and hating, and so enter into and remain within the depressive position (Klein 1975c). Nevertheless, the thesis that the child's hatred and destructiveness is innate, unrelated, at least at first, to the quality of the child's relationship with its mother and others, leaves even some sympathetic followers cold. As Meira Likierman puts it,

To attribute destructive impulses to the infant was one thing; it was quite another to propose a curious anti-life tendency which underpins attacks on the very mothering resources that are essential to mental growth. (Likierman 2001, 177)[3]

---

[3] Simon Clarke (2004) helped me understand how radical Klein's concept of envy and the death-drive truly is, both in his article and in conversation. D. W. Winnicott cannot abide Klein's thesis, writing in "Hate in the Counter Transference" that "the mother hates the baby before the baby hates the mother, and before the baby can know his mother hates him" (Winnicott 1978, 73). If this is so, then we must rethink the "death instinct," seeing it as a response to real relationships, including the relationship of being hated.

If one allows oneself to think about it for very long, Klein's version of the *Todestrieb* is even more troubling than Freud's, as it seeks not even the pleasure of Nirvana, but the destruction of the good that makes even one's own life and growth possible. The only character who comes close to such an awful thesis is Milton's Satan. This is true whether Satan's rage is directed against his benevolent creator God precisely *because* He is generous and kind, asking so little in return (*Paradise Lost* IV, 43–55) or whether Satan's rage is directed against the mutual love and respect of Adam and Eve before the Fall. Satan is not simply jealous; for he would not have sex with Eve even if he could, eventually procreating Sin and Death out of himself. Rather, Satan simply cannot abide the very existence of such a pure and perfect love as that between Adam and Eve (PL IV, 505–508). What Klein calls envy, the desire to destroy the good because it is good, comes closer to Satan's desire.

Klein draws a sharp distinction between jealousy and envy. We must do the same in order to think clearly about evil. In jealousy, I want to possess goods that belong to you because I don't have them, such as a beautiful spouse, or a lovely house. In envy, I don't want what you have, perhaps because I already have a beautiful spouse and lovely house of my own. Rather, I want to spoil what you have because the very existence of you enjoying these goods makes me feel less good. For me to feel good, you must feel bad. As Chaucer puts it in a passage quoted by Klein (1975c, 189), envy is the worst sin because it opposes life and creativity itself.

It is certain that envy is the worst sin that is; for all other sins are sins only against one virtue, whereas envy is against all virtue and against all goodness.

Klein might have continued to quote Chaucer, who goes on to say that envy "is sorry for all the goodness of one's neighbor, making it different from all other sins. There is scarcely any sin that doesn't have within it some delight, but Envy has within it only anguish and sorrow" (*Canterbury Tales*, "The Parson's Tale," 485–490).[4]

Only Klein, I believe, allows us to fully appreciate the lust to destroy the innocent and good. Only a natural law that takes this perverted

---

[4] Klein (1975c, 189) does not give the source for her translation into modern English. Mine is Chaucer 1993, 536.

lust seriously has a chance of making sense of this benighted world, for only then do see why we must we put reparation for all the destruction we have witnessed, caused, or imagined at the center of moral life. But perhaps Freud said it best after all, drawing even the ancient gods into this conflict.

And now, I think, the meaning of the evolution of civilization is no longer obscure to us. It must present the struggle between Eros and Death, between the instinct of life and the instinct of destruction, as it works itself out in the human species. This struggle is what all life essentially consists of, and the evolution of civilization may therefore be simply described as the struggle for life of the human species. And it is this battle of the giants that our nurse-maids try to appease with their lullaby about Heaven. (Freud 1930, 121–122)

Let us not let natural law become one more lullaby.

THE PRIVATION OF GOOD: AUGUSTINE, ARENDT, AND MELANIE KLEIN

Is it a lullaby to imagine that the world we live in is good? Can one authentically and naively experience the goodness of the world as Augustine once did?

Certainly you love only the good, because the earth is good by the height of its mountains . . . and good is the house that is arranged through in symmetrical proportions and is spacious and bright . . . and good is the mild and salubrious air . . . and good is health without pains and weariness . . . and good is the countenance of man with regular features, a cheerful expression, and a glowing color; and good is the soul of a friend with the sweetness of concord and the fidelity of love; and good is the just man; and good are riches because they readily assist us; and good is the heaven with is own sun, moon and stars . . . and good is the poem with its measured rhythm and seriousness of thoughts. (*On the Trinity*, book 8, c. 3, 4)

For Augustine, the world and everything that in it is good, for the world is made by God. "Every creature of God is good," says Paul to Timothy (1 Tim. 4:4), a passage cited by Aquinas to make the same point as Augustine: evil does not exist, except as the privation of the good (*Summa Contra Gentiles*, book 3, part 1, c. 4).

Theodor Adorno wrote that it is barbaric to write poetry after Auschwitz (Adorno 1983, 34). Later Adorno said that he meant only lyric poetry, and perhaps that still goes too far. Nevertheless, one wonders whether one can read Augustine's paean to the world's goodness in quite the same way after Auschwitz. Writing in *Auschwitz: Beginning of a New Era?* Irving Greenberg (1977, 23) frames the issue even more sharply. "No statement, theological or otherwise, should be made that would not be credible in the presence of burning children."

Doesn't Augustine's insistence on seeing only the world's goodness look more like blindness after almost two thousand years of bloody history, culminating in the terrible twentieth century, the bloodiest in world history? Yet, one who contemplated the horror of the Holocaust more thoughtfully than most, Hannah Arendt, seems deeply influenced by Augustine's view of evil as the privation of the good. Indeed, privation seems to inspire what she calls the banality of evil. Recently, several critics of Arendt have made this connection. This will come as no surprise to those who know Arendt's work. As late at the early 1960s, Arendt was revising her 1929 dissertation, *Der Liebesbegriff bei Augustin*, for publication.

If one sees privation as a more active concept of evil than is generally recognized, akin to Klein's account of spoiling the good because it is good, and not me or mine, then the banality of evil also appears in a different light. Consider a familiar example used by countless generations of teachers to explain Augustine's view of evil, that of a lovely garment spoiled by a rent in the fabric. The tear in the fabric is nothing substantial. On the contrary, the hole has the quality of nothingness where something good should be. That's what Augustine means by evil, or so countless teachers have taught their students. Is it compatible with Augustine to take this example one step further, arguing that evil is the deliberate rending of the fabric, the intentional destruction of the beautiful and good because it is beautiful and good? If so, then the evil that Augustine writes about comes close to the *Todestrieb*, the death drive, understood as sadism, envy, and destruction. And if this reading is compatible with Augustine, could it be compatible with Arendt?

At about the same time as she was revising her dissertation on Augustine, Arendt covered the trial of Adolf Eichmann in Jerusalem for *The New Yorker* magazine. Though the Holocaust may have been the product of a single evil mind, it required thousands of willing conspirators to carry it out. Few were more important than Eichmann, who organized the transfer of Jews to the death camps. It was Arendt's experience listening to and watching Eichmann day after day that led her to formulate her controversial concept of the banality of evil.

Is there a connection between privation and banality? Joanna Scott and Judith Stark (1966, 120) think there is, arguing that "Augustine's understanding of evil as habituated *cupiditas* may thus have passed over the bridge of her 1929 dissertation to her own notorious analysis of Eichmann's evil as 'banal.'" Trouble is, even if Arendt's concept of the banality of evil is traced back to Augustine, this does not make either one of them correct. Neither privation nor banality seem adequate explanations of the terrible things that men and women do to each other, the organized humiliation, brutalization, torture, and murder of millions, to say nothing of our everyday cruelties. But, perhaps this depends on how we understand the terms privation and banality. Nothing binds us to the understanding of their originators, Augustine and Arendt, as long as one specifies where one goes off in a different direction, and why. Furthermore, Augustine particularly is not always so clear about what he means by privation (*privatio*). This, it turns out, is good, not bad.

While Arendt does seem to draw her concept of the banality of evil from Augustine's concept of evil as privation, there is a subtle richness, or perhaps I should say contradictoriness, in Augustine's account that is missing in Arendt.

Augustine was about sixteen when he pilfered the famous pears. Earlier, when still a child, he tells us, he stole food from the family larder. He knew it was wrong, but he understood the motive. The food was a bribe, used to get other children to play with him. Later he would commit what he came to regard as sexual sin. But it was the theft of the pears that disturbed him most.

Coming home one night with some friends, they stole into in a farmer's orchard and carted off a load of pears. Augustine didn't want the pears. He had better pears at home. Eventually he and his friends dumped some of the pears before swine. Why did they do it? Augustine wonders if he stole the pears out of the pleasure of transgression itself. Was it an *acte gratuit*? "Simply what was not allowed allured us" (*Confessions* II.iii.9).

In his *Confessions*, Augustine writes in the same vein as Aquinas (ST I, 49), arguing that people do bad things in the pursuit of an apparent good. But stealing the pears pursued no good at all. Could that be in some way worse than murder?

> A murder is committed. Why? To get another's wife or wealth, or to get the necessities of life. Or for fear another would deprive the murderer of such things. Or from a sense of wrong burning for redress. Who murders with no cause but to enjoy the mere murdering? Who would credit such a motive? (*Confessions* II.III.9)

Stealing pears isn't murder, but Augustine is as troubled over his motive as if it were. As he rejects the possibility of pleasure in murder for its own sake, for the pleasure of the destruction of life, Augustine finally rejects the possibility of pleasure in theft, done for its own sake. Even the brutal and cruel Catiline, of whom Sallust said that he was evil and savage without reason, had a rational motive: to keep in practice, lest he be slow to react when attacked. Augustine concludes, "No, not even Catiline [Lucius Sergius Catilina] himself loved his crimes; something else motivated him to commit them" (*Confessions* II.V.11). Is not Augustine working a little too hard to make Catiline's savagery a rational act, perverse but nonetheless based on reason?

Augustine's view of evil as privation is neither shallow nor banal. Evil as the privation of good implies not merely the absence of good, but an absence stemming from an act of self-assertion in which one makes one's own will absolute, so that the good begins and ends with me. Or as Alasdair MacIntyre puts it about Augustine's concept of evil, "Augustine sees the evil of human nature in the consent which the will gives to evil ... Evil is somehow or other such and the human will is somehow or other such that the will can delight in evil" (MacIntyre 1981, 163).

Perhaps this is the key. If one sees evil as privation, as an act of making one's own will absolute, an act that has hardened into a second nature, so to speak, then one has created a world in which the good begins and ends with me. Here is another context in which to read Satan's original act of self-assertion: "Evil be thou my good." In this statement, Satan makes his will the alpha and the omega, the beginning and the end of all that exists. This tendency is only exacerbated in the modern world.

While one might talk about this phenomenon of the absolutization of the will in terms of the culture of narcissism, as Christopher Lasch

(1979) called it, one could as readily talk about it in the language of evil. A way of being in the world that knows (and wishes to know) no connection between one's life, one's acts, and the suffering of others may itself be evil. Extreme thoughtlessness may itself be evil, even if Arendt's explanation for it, what she calls the banality of evil, is inadequate. This is the direction my argument is heading, even if it will take a while to get there. First it will be necessary to define evil, or at least to make the attempt.

What's Evil?

An Old Testament term often translated as evil, *ra^c*, refers to anything bad, displeasing, or harmful to man. Evil is not just what one does, but what one suffers (Isa. 45:7; Jer. 4:6; Amos 3:6; Mic. 2:3; Eccles. 1:13; Job 2:10). Nor is this original meaning confined to the Old Testament. The New Testament term often translated as evil, *kakía*, means whatever is bad, such as pain, sickness, suffering, misfortune, and loss. Certainly both Augustine and Aquinas, who wrote almost a thousand years later, see evil as a deficiency in an otherwise good nature.

Morally bad people occur infrequently in Aquinas. Even the German robbers are far from wholly bad, observing many of the natural laws, such as caring for their children (ST I–II, 94, 4, 6). There is, in other words, nothing Satanic about the German robbers, even as Aquinas uses terms like "evil habit" to characterize them. Aquinas' typical example of evil is much more likely to be drawn from nature, such as the otherwise healthy man with a twisted leg (Aquinas, *Summa Contra Gentiles*, book 3, part 1, c. 10).

Fascinating about Augustine is that while he holds a doctrine of evil similar to that of Aquinas (not surprising, since Augustine formulated it first), Augustine struggles with counterexamples that don't fit his definition. The most famous is his theft of the pears. As Plato is drawn to the Eros which so frightens him (compare *The Gorgias* and *The Republic* with the *Symposium* and *Phaedrus*), so the younger Augustine is fascinated with the activity of evil whose very activity he must deny in order to preserve God's perfect goodness.[5]

---

[5] Toward the end of his life, Augustine became less interested in evil. His teachings on predestination have the effect of making even good will a gift of God. From this

I am going to define evil as Milton's Satan does when he says "Evil be thou my Good" (PL IV, 105–110). Were Augustine magically able to read Milton, he might well say "See, what did I tell you! No one pursues evil for its own sake. They pursue the good about which they are mistaken." Were Augustine magically able to read a contemporary author, he might find confirmation in Jean-Paul Sartre's remark that no one ever does evil without first calling it good (Sartre 1999, 37).

I'm going to read Milton differently. "Evil be thou my Good," taken in the context of Satan's project, means that Satan would take revenge on God *because* He is good, *because* His rule was mild and loving (PL IV, 43). Satan does not just envy God's power; he envies His goodness. Says Satan,

I ... thought one step higher would set me highest, and in a moment quit the debt immense of endless gratitude, so burdensome still, paying still to owe; forgetful what from Him I still received. (PL IV, 50–55)

In old English "quit" means requite, or to take revenge.

Here is the real meaning of evil, and the only one to get it right is Melanie Klein, even as she chooses Chaucer instead of Milton to make her point. Evil is an attack on the good precisely because it is good and not me or mine. It is this that Milton's Satan cannot stand, and Augustine cannot quite let himself know, even as he comes so terribly close. Aquinas, so like Aristotle to Augustine's Plato, cannot even begin to let himself think this unthinkable thought. There is, in other words, a clarity about evil in Aquinas that makes his work on this topic less rich and interesting. A similar clarity exists in Arendt, and I do not mean this as praise.

Evil as privation is by no means merely an absence or lack of goodness. Privation involves a willing identification with evil. Nevertheless, Augustine's view lacks the distinctly Kleinian sense of evil: the spoiling and destruction of the good because it is good and not me or mine, the hatred of goodness itself. Not even in Catiline can Augustine find that. Augustine sets *caritas* against *cupiditas*, brotherly and sisterly love against cupidity. Klein, like Freud, sets Eros against Thanatos, and that

perspective, human evil is insignificant, no more than a gnat bite, when measured against God's grace (Evans 1982, xi, 149). My concern is primarily with Augustine's earlier, but post-Manichean, thinking about evil.

is really the difference. When he says "Evil be thou my Good," Milton's Satan comes closer to Freud and Klein than Augustine (PL IV, 105–110).

Coming at this question from the opposite direction, could one argue that the envious spoiling of the good is similar to Augustine's precept of privation? Both would render the good less than wholly good without putting anything substantial in its place. In that way envious spoiling and privation are similar. Nevertheless, a will to destruction of the good exists in envious spoiling that is absent in Augustine's account, even if it is hinted at in the story of the pears.

The will to evil that Augustine discovers in himself is the will to transgress for its own sake, and the perverse pleasure in being wicked that goes with it. "Simply what was not allowed allured us (*eo liberet quo non liceret*)" (*Confessions* II.iv.9–II.vi.13). Taking pleasure in being bad may sound evil, and perhaps it is. Still, there is something adolescent in the way being bad thrills Augustine (as one might expect of a sixteen year old), who says "I loved the self-destruction, I loved my fall, not the object for which I had fallen but my fall itself" (*Confessions* II.iv.9). One could perhaps argue that the good Augustine would destroy is his own, and perhaps that is so, but the tone of this passage is not that of envious spoiling, but the thrill of transgression. If this is evil, it is of a lesser order.

As he rejects the possibility of pleasure in murder for its own sake, for the pleasure of the destruction of life, Augustine finally rejects the possibility of pleasure in theft, done for its own sake. Puzzling long and hard over his larceny, Augustine concludes that it had something to do with his friends, that he wouldn't have done it alone. Could "bonding" with his friends, as it is called today, have been the reason, the apparent good that justifies the bad (*Confessions* II.viii.16)?[6] Augustine appears content with this answer, reflecting no further, even as he seems to sense that his answer is inadequate, that he has crossed a threshold of moral possibility (the love of destruction for its own sake) but is unable to go further. Aquinas does not go half as far (ST I–II, 71, 2).

---

[6] Kenneth Burke suggests that the band of boys who stole the pears "form a blasphemous counterpart to the fellowship of the Christian Church, in that the *gratuitousness* of the sin that binds them together is balanced and redeemed by Christ's gift of *grace* to all who accept the offer of salvation through its blood" (Rudnytsky 1994, 138, author's emphasis; I quote Rudnytsky).

My explanation of Augustine's theft is not the only psychoanalytic interpretation around. On the contrary, Augustine's pears are a popular topic for psychoanalytic reflection. Peter Rudnytsky sees Augustine's recollection of the theft of the pears as a "screen memory," as Freud called it, in which "everyday and indifferent events" take the place of "serious and tragic ones" (Freud 1899, 305; Rudnytsky 1994). And what does the theft screen? Augustine's Oedipal desire for his mother, Monica, with whom he had an intensely close relationship. Rudnytsky's strongest argument is "the disproportion between the triviality of Augustine's offense and the extreme importance he attaches to it." This disproportion

> may thus be explained psychoanalytically as a displacement of the sense of guilt attaching itself to the former events [his desire for his mother] onto the latter. It is this displacement of affect from something serious onto something trivial that makes the theft of the pears truly a 'screen memory.' (Rudnytsky 1994, 140)

Rudnytsky could be correct. This is one of those questions whose answer is impossible to know. What we are talking about, in any case, is not simply how close an interpretation comes to reality, but what the interpretation allows us to do. Rudnytsky's allows us to see the theft of the pears not just as an Oedipal displacement, but as trope that connects two primordial sins: the Original Sin that led to the Fall with Oedipal guilt. As Augustine remarks in *The City of God*, the lure of the forbidden fruit for Adam (as for Augustine) was that it was forbidden (XIV.12). Indeed, Augustine refers to the pears as *poma*, the same term used in the Latin Vulgate Bible to refer to the fruit in the Garden of Eden (Rudnytsky 1994, 138–138).

My interpretation, on the other hand, allows us to take Augustine at his word: that he really is troubled and puzzled by the thrill of transgression for its own sake. It is this, and the problem of evil that it represents that so vexes Augustine. When in doubt about a person's motives, it is not the worst principle to take him at his word, a principle I tried to follow with informants. Not perhaps, as the last word, but the first, in this case that Augustine is truly puzzled about what he claims to be puzzled about, his pleasure in destruction for its own sake. In any case, Augustine's reference to the brutality of Catiline, his desperate attempt to make Catiline's savagery rational, fits only my account. (One could make something oedipal of the fact that it was Catiline's mistress who betrayed him to Cicero, but to make this the unconscious significance of Augustine's reference to Catiline seems a stretch.)

Perhaps one should let Rudnytsky have the last word after all. "Just as the oedipal patterns in Augustine's life as a whole are superimposed upon preoedipal ones, so his theft of the pears is open to interpretations on multiple psychological levels" (Rudnytsky 1994, 140). Klein always understood that oedipal desire begins in the savage desire to possess the contents of mother's body, and so perhaps there is not so much difference between Klein and Freud here. In fact, this is the context of Glover's remark that Klein is a theorist of original sin (Klein 1975a; Rudnytsky 1994, 46). Since Rudnytsky has already linked Freud's account of the oedipal conflict with Original Sin, the connection to Klein is transitive, so to speak.

While one is tempted to give Rudnytsky the last word, there is one more possibility to consider, one that fits neither Rudnytsky's categories nor my own, at least not neatly. If evil refers not just to what one does, but to what one suffers, then another way of thinking about Augustine's view of evil as privation suggests itself. Evil as deprivation, the loss of all one cares about, all that makes life worth living. Augustine was remarkably sensitive to this experience, writing of the death of his friend.

My eyes look for him everywhere, and he was not there. I hated everything because they did not have him, nor could they now tell me 'look, he is on the way,' as used to be the case when he was alive and absent from me.... I was surprised that any other mortals were alive.... I was even more surprised that when he was dead I was alive. (*Confessions*, 4.9)

Seen from this perspective, evil as privation is not simply the absence of the good. It is the loss of one who seems to embody all goodness. Elaine Pagels, author of *The Origin of Satan*, writes that the book was composed under the impress of the loss of her husband, and shortly thereafter her son (Pagels 1995, 184). If we see evil as privation as a way of talking about human loss, then evil itself begins to make more sense. Evil is the loss of everything that makes life worth living, an experience so awesome and awful that it must be attributed to malevolent forces, lest life itself be emptied of meaning, and goodness rendered void. What Klein adds is the desperate fear that this malevolent force might be located inside oneself, the hate we harbor for those we love. Evil is, in other words, the experience of loss in the paranoid-schizoid dimension. With this too natural law must deal.

While natural law must deal with this dimension of evil, let us not use it as an excuse to forget our fundamental argument. Evil is not merely an experience of loss, though it is that too. Evil is pleasure in the destruction of the good because it is good, the corruption of innocence because it is innocent. Perhaps the experience of the loss of all goodness in the world becomes an experience of evil in the paranoid-schizoid dimension because in a secret part of ourselves (secret sometimes even to ourselves) we are intimately acquainted with the devil who would destroy goodness for its own sake. On this sobering thought, let us turn to Hannah Arendt's account of the trial of Adolf Eichmann.

From Augustine to Arendt and Back Again

Arendt's report on Eichmann's trial remains controversial to this day, as Arendt seemed to say that Eichmann was such a banal bureaucrat that he never truly thought about what he was doing, murdering millions of Jews. Indeed, this is what puzzles Arendt so. How could pale little men do such awful deeds, the murder of millions? In coming to terms with this fact, Arendt says that she had to give up her former belief in radical evil.

It is indeed my opinion now that evil is never "radical," that it is only extreme, and that it possesses neither depth nor any demonic dimension. It can overgrow and lay waste the whole world precisely because it spreads like a fungus on the surface. It [evil] is "thought-defying," as I said, because thought tries to reach some depth, to go to the roots, and the moment it concerns itself with evil, it is frustrated because there is nothing. That is its 'banality.' Only the good has depth and can be radical (Elshtain 1995, 76).[7]

Arendt, by the way, never denied the existence of radical evil in the abstract, in theory. If we understand radical evil as malevolence and hate, then Arendt found it in such fictional characters as Iago and

---

[7] The passage is from an "acrimonious exchange" between Arendt and Gershom Scholem (Elshtain 1995, 76). Anyone familiar with Elshtain's *Augustine and the Limits of Politics* (1995) will know how much I owe to her work, even if I do not always follow her argument.

Macbeth (Arendt 1965, 229). Not the existence of radical evil, but its absence in Eichmann and his collaborators, is Arendt's position.

Earlier, in *The Origins of Totalitarianism*, Arendt characterized the last stages of totalitarianism as "absolute evil." "If it is true that in the final stages of totalitarianism an absolute evil appears (absolute because it can no longer be deduced from comprehensively human motives), it is also true that without it we might never have known the truly radical nature of evil." (Arendt 1973, ix). Though Arendt did not elaborate, the concept of radical evil struck a chord, even as it was Immanuel Kant who first used the term.[8]

In *Eichmann in Jerusalem*, Arendt (1965) does not change what she thinks about evil. Evil is still defined in terms of its incomprehensibility, what she now calls "thought defying." What changes is her judgment about what makes evil thought defying – that it possesses no qualities to think about. Indeed, one might argue that not even this changed, just the location of evil, so to speak, from deeply rooted to on the surface.

Behind Arendt's reformulation of evil was her determination not to permit Eichmann or any of his fellow Nazis to attain the status of dramatic or romantic demiurges. They must be shown to be who they really were: limited, hollowed-out, pale and empty men. This is the banality of evil. Especially important for Arendt was to strip evil of its generative power. Above all, evil cannot be creative; evil cannot be allowed to bring anything new into the world (Elshtain 1995, 84–85).

Surely Arendt is onto something; her program of destroying the legend of the greatness of evil is a worthwhile project. William Blake's *bon mot*, that Satan gets all the best lines in *Paradise Lost*, should remind us that there is something attractive about evil, and that should worry us. Something akin to this way of thinking lies behind Augustine's

[8] For Kant, radical evil is a defect (*malum defectus*) not of reason but of will, which transforms morality into the servant of desire, so that we can do what we want with a good conscience. The similarity to Augustine's concept of evil as the absolutization of my will is striking. Like Augustine, Kant excludes in advance the possibility that someone would want to destroy the good because it is good, for that would assume "a thoroughly evil will . . . and thus the subject would be a devilish being. Neither of these designations is applicable to man" (Kant 1960, 30–32). Evidently some possibilities are just too horrible to consider. Which does not, unfortunately, make it impossible that these possibilities exist.

concerns as well: only God is great; only God is creative and fruitful. Evil just is, the absence of goodness and fecundity. Real procreativity takes a relationship with another. Not only that, but whereas for Augustine God is abstract, everywhere and not diluted, evil is concrete, and tied to bodies (ST I, 48, 1–2). In a related fashion, Klein characterizes the nadir of the paranoid-schizoid position in terms of the inability to abstract symbols from the bodies that they represent (Klein 1975f).

The equation of body and symbol in torture is an extreme instance of the identification of signifier and signified. Evidence for this claim is found in the way torture it is so often represented as the drama it is not. It is, I believe, no accident that the torture chamber is called the "production room" in the Philippines, the "cinema room" in South Vietnam, and the "blue lit stage" in Chile" (Scarry 1985, 28). But the language is a lie. In drama, a transformed larger world is acted out on a small stage. In torture, the world is reduced to the body of the victim. In creation we animate the world, bringing the dead material world to life with the spirit of body and mind. Torture is reverse animism, reducing the world to the human body. Rather than nonbody symbolizing body, body comes to symbolize a world reduced to its bare essentials, pain and power. How strange that even the term "symbolize" could become a lie, but that is what happens, suggesting a degree of abstraction not present in torture. It is not that the body comes to symbolize the world: the body becomes the world, is the world.

Though Arendt understands something important about evil, aspects of her project are troubling. It is as if the goal of showing that evil cannot be great (even greatly evil and terrible) is so important that something of the horror of the evil gets lost: that behind evil lies the will to destroy the pure, the innocent and the good because the other is pure, innocent, and good, and the evildoer is not. It is this that Milton's Satan grasps, the same point that Augustine comes so close to seeing before turning away.

Let me suggest another way of thinking about evil and evil doers, along the lines of the cliché "way down deep he's shallow." Admittedly, the Nazis were shallow men, but that does not mean their evil was shallow. On the contrary, it is because they were shallow men that their evil ran so deep. Evil may be deep even as evil doers are generally (always?) shallow. To make evil deep is not to glorify it, only to suggest that evil is a force that transcends (as the unconscious transcends) the awareness of those who practice it.

At about this point the thoughtful reader may be asking "what is this deep and shallow business anyway? What sort of intuitive but vague distinction does it represent?" One result of the Freudian revolution was to see that even the most ordinary man has a creative unconscious, expressed for example in dreams. Even the most boring bureaucratic may have fantastic phantasies. Phillip Rieff makes this same point when he says "Freud democratized genius by giving everyone a creative unconscious" (Rieff 1961, 36). Banal Nazi bureaucrats likely possessed an extraordinary unconscious, filled with phantasies of hate and destruction, as well as perverse urges to purify the world. That these men and women, like Eichmann, may not have been aware of their destructive phantasies, that they may have deeply repressed them, does not mean that these phantasies were not present. On the contrary, the more repressed the phantasy, the greater (not the lesser) power it has over its possessor, as the possessor has no opportunity to exercise rational control over what he knows nothing. It is incorrect to say that the motivation of someone like Eichmann is shallow. Eichmann may be shallow, but his motivation is deep – as deep as the hating human heart, and the most destructive human phantasy.

Evil may run deep, even as those in whom it runs deep are shallow and banal, unaware of the world of death and destruction that lies within. Perhaps it is the very shallowness of their understanding that makes them more vulnerable to the acting out of these phantasies when they become socially sanctioned, as was the case under the Nazis. Indeed, in these circumstances we might even be justified in talking about a collective destructive unconscious, though precisely what that might mean remains obscure. Perhaps just that the ideology of the times encouraged and channeled the destructive phantasies of millions in a similar direction, as though to socialize phantasy itself.

Alice Miller gives an example of what this might mean.

I know a woman who never happened to have any contact with a Jew up to the time she joined the *Bund Deutscher Mädel*, the female equivalent of the Hitler Youth. She had been brought up very strictly. Her parents needed her to help out in the household after her siblings (two brothers and a sister) had left home. . . . Much later she told me with what enthusiasm she had read about 'the crimes of the Jews' in *Mein Kampf* and what a sense of relief it had given her to find out that it was permissible to hate someone so unequivocally. She had never been allowed to envy her siblings openly for being able to pursue their careers. . . . And now, quite unexpectedly, there was such a simple solution: it was all right to hate as much as she wanted; she still remained (and perhaps for this reason was) her parents' good girl and a useful daughter of the fatherland. (Miller 1983, 64)

While it may be correct to argue that evil is not creative, reducing the world to the dimensions of pain, suffering, and destruction, one wants to be careful about employing aesthetic categories, such as creativity, to moral debate. Is the good always creative? Sometimes the good itself is boring, and mundane, the tedious work of feeding the hungry, and clothing the poor, including victims who are not always ennobled by their victimhood. Why make creativity the issue one way or the other? Is it not enough to say that evil is bad and should be avoided, whereas goodness is good and should be pursued?

Why is creativity so important to Arendt? Because she sees the act of bringing something new into the world, what she calls natality, as the only alternative to bureaucracy, totalitarianism, and the banality of evil. Indeed, for Arendt, bureaucracy itself is virtually a form of totalitarianism: in both the individual disappears, or rather becomes superfluous. In a letter written in the month that *The Origins of Total-itarianism* was published, Arendt says "What radical evil really is, I don't know, but it has something to do with [this] phenomenon: the superfluity of men as men" (Young-Bruehl 1982, 255; McGowan 1998, 30–31) This is also the goal of bureaucracy, what the phrase "like cogs in a machine" means when it refers to bureaucracy: not that people are not needed to man and woman the bureaucracy, but that one can readily be replaced by another as they are all alike. Bureaucracy is the principle of the factory, the division of labor, applied to the manufacture of decisions.

If totalitarianism and bureaucracy are both characterized by the superfluity of the individual, then the link to the banality of evil becomes clear, for that is precisely what characterizes the evil of men like Eichmann, "desk murderers" (*Schreibtischmörder*) as they are rightly called in German. Eichmann was not acting as an individual; he did not even think about himself as an individual, except perhaps when questions of promotion were concerned, and even then it was his place in the system that mattered. Eichmann conceived of himself as superfluous. Totalitarianism, radical evil, bureaucracy, and the banality of evil are all of a piece: in each of them the individual disappears, and with his or her disappearance comes an inability to think about what one is doing.

Here is the connection between Augustine and Arendt on the problem of evil. Or so it seems. About this connection, Elshtain states in a book first published in 1995 that "it is surprising to me that, at this late date, no one . . . in that vast cottage industry that is Arendt studies has made the connection . . . between Arendt's banality of evil and Augustine's" view of evil as privation (Elshtain 1995, 77). This neglect did not last long. In their interpretative essay accompanying their collation of Arendt's dissertation, *Love and Saint Augustine*, Joanna Scott and Judith Stark state that as Arendt

argued in her dissertation and more concretely in the Eichmann study, surrender to habituated behavior, and the resulting avoidance of responsibility, define the death of free will and moral judgment – Augustine's sin of *cupiditas*. It was not love of the world as such which was wrong, but the resulting failure to 'think what we are doing,' or failing to do, as a result. . . . The Eichmann trial presented the problem of 'thoughtlessness' as an operational definition of evil. (Scott and Stark 1996, 191–193)

Here is the obvious place to stop, the thread that connects Augustine's view of evil with that of Arendt made clear for all to see. Yet, there is a problem. Augustine's view of evil is, I have argued, richer than his concept. One cannot say the same about Arendt's banality of evil. To be sure, Arendt's concept is suggestive, particularly in the way it makes thoughtlessness, rather than malignancy, central to evil. Nevertheless, we need to understand thoughtlessness better, and Arendt is not helpful.

Arendt is unhelpful not because she resists psychological speculation (often that is the best course, especially among the psychologically uninclined), but because thoughtlessness, superficiality, banality, and evil come to mutually define each other in a way that is unilluminating. Thoughtlessness isn't just the "operational definition" of evil; thoughtlessness becomes the very essence of evil, at least by default. This doesn't make Arendt wrong. It means that we must devote more time to thinking about thoughtlessness. That is what I propose to do next.

THOUGHT AND THOUGHTLESSNESS

Let us approach thoughtlessness not as banality, but as irony. Let us explore the hidden depths beneath the superficial shallowness of one who does evil without thinking – indeed, without being able to think – about what he or she is doing, or acts' consequences. Let us explore evil as the destruction of thought itself, the death drive unknowingly directed against knowledge. In so doing we shall come to understand better how Arendt came so late to Satan's party, confusing evil with the destruction evil has wrought.

Recall how Likierman (2001, 177) characterizes the death drive in Klein, as an attack on those mothering resources (let us just call it mother love, though in some cases it might as well be father love or grandmother love) that makes mental growth possible. Developing this insight at length, it is Klein's student, Wilfred Bion (1989), who made the inability to think the great puzzle of psychoanalysis.[9]

Perhaps it should be the great puzzle of philosophy as well. We assume that thought is difficult, the product of great minds. What if thought, understood as thinking about what we are doing and to whom we are doing it, is at once the easiest and most difficult task in the world? Almost anyone can do it, but most people, as well as entire societies, are organized to defend against it, a point Aquinas seems to recognize when he posits "shun ignorance" (*ignorantiam vitet*) as a leading inference of the natural law. To say that thinking is natural, but not necessarily common, is consistent with how Aquinas, indeed how most, have traditionally thought about the precepts of the natural law. Natural doesn't mean easy. Natural means to do something that defines a uniquely human existence well, such as thinking. This takes tutoring and practice, which is why the development of natural athletic ability is a good analogy.

Bion's answer to why some can't think was what he called attacks on linking. It's easy to have thoughts. The trick is to know how to put them

---

[9] Klein first saw psychoanalysis as an account of failed thought and failed symbolism, both the result of the intense aggression associated with the desire to know, the epistemophilic impulse as Klein calls it (1975a). Bion developed what was begun in Klein. The exact status of Bion among the Kleinians is a subject of much dispute, none of which matters here. R. D. Hinshelwood (1989, 229–234) discusses the issue succinctly and well.

together, what is called thinking, without being overwhelmed with terror or despair. Attacks on linking seem to stem from hatred of thought itself, a hatred of knowing what one is feeling. What is puzzling, or at least surprising, is why Bion, and to a lesser degree Likierman, would connect a hatred of emotion with a hatred of thought. Why, for instance, would Likierman, say that the death drive attacks the mother love that makes mental growth possible? One might have expected her to say that the death drive attacks the mother love that makes emotional security or autonomy possible. In fact, for many post-Kleinians they amount to the same thing.

Inspired by Bion, post-Kleinians focus on the destruction of thought for reasons that run something like this.[10] What children and adults need, albeit in different degrees and in different ways, is for their unbearable emotions to be held and contained by another. What are unbearable emotions? Emotions that feel as if the self is going to fall to pieces or explode, for the emotions are so intense, unstable, and unintegrated into the self. If mother contains the young child's unbearable emotions ten thousand times, eventually the young child will learn to do this emotional work for him or herself, a process that might be thought of as internalizing the maternal holding function so as to make it one's own.

At first, mother contains these emotions simply by showing that she can experience them without retaliating or falling to pieces. Later she may help the child put words to these emotions, such as "You look so angry that you're about to burst." This must be said in a way that neither trivializes nor overdramatizes the emotion, as if to say "but of course you're not going to burst, so let's get on with making dinner."

Attacks on linking occur when there is a failure of containment and holding. The attack on linking is the fragmenting alternative to being held, in which the unbearable emotions are broken into pieces, disconnected from thoughts, so that thoughts become sterile,

---

[10] My primary sources are Bion's essays "Attacks on Linking" (93–109) and "A Theory of Thinking" (110–119) both in his *Second Thoughts* (1984). Also helpful was his *Learning From Experience* (1989, 89–99), which introduces the minus K, or anti-Knowledge link: not just the desire to destroy the links between thoughts, but the desire to destroy knowledge itself. Among other authors on this topic, Herbert Rosenfeld (1988) and John Steiner (1993) stand out.

one-dimensional, bereft of the emotions that would invigorate thoughts and give them life, only in this case life is too terrifying, too close to death. The result of attacks on linking is thinking marked by a lack of curiosity, a hatred of emotions, and from there it is but a short step to hatred of life itself. Emotions are what give life the feeling of living, not just existing. But when emotions are too intense and frightening, such as rage at and terror of abandonment, emotions are experienced as an alien intrusion into the self. An emotion or feeling itself becomes a hostile attacker that – if it cannot be destroyed – must be severed from all meaning.

Why? For the same reason that Milton's Satan would be his own progenitor, wrenching himself from the earth to be born, entirely self-caused. Lusting after Eve, Satan will nonetheless not have intercourse with her, because to do so would be to desire her, and so to be emotionally affected (linked) to another, if only for a moment. Instead, Satan procreates Sin and Death out of himself, children of incest and his own imagination. (PL IX, 480–495) Satan will not accept the most fundamental reality of all, the emotional reality of others, the emotional claim of others upon our lives: that the existence of others whom we want, need, desire, or pity invades the sanctum sanctorum of our inner world, causing us to feel. Attacks on linking are an attempt to protect this inner sanctum from the invasion of feeling that feels as if it cannot be contained.

Bion argues that emotions come to be experienced as an attack on one's primary narcissism: "I am the world." This fits Satan, but in general it is probably more accurate to say that emotions remind us of how much we depend on others outside ourselves. Attacks on linking are an attempt to abolish one's dependence on a world of others. In the end, of course, there is not much difference between these two ways of putting it. The advantage of the latter way is only that we need not posit a hypothetical state of primary narcissism, but only that people need each other far more than most of us can bear to know.

Attacks on linking are attacks on emotions, or rather on the links between emotions and their objects. Short circuit this link, and the emotion loses the emotional energy that feeds it. So too does thought, which becomes dry, withered, abstract. It is this state that Antoine Roquentin, the protagonist in Jean-Paul Sartre's novel *Nausea*, longs to recover but can't, instead feeling overwhelmed by the insistent particularity of the world. "I would have liked [the world] to exist less strongly, more dryly, in a more abstract way" (Sartre 1964, 127).

Reality is a suspect term these days, almost as suspect as the term nature. More useful perhaps is to focus on the lie. Lies reign in Pandemonium, where Satan rules and waits in exile. Only they don't look or sound like lies. Lies look and sound like productivity. Pandemonium is the busiest place around, its residents always building, marching, celebrating, and preparing for war (PL I.717–719). In many respects, we live in Pandemonium today. Busy, busy, busy, all in the service of not stopping long enough to know what we are feeling and doing, as it is this knowledge itself that is unbearable. Put this passionate ignorance together with an insight into what one is really doing in that telluric, prepolitical space in which Steiner locates Antigone's connection to the natural law – hopelessly confusing Eros and Thanatos, being and nonbeing, life and death – and one has a view of human history that aspires to tragedy. The tragedy of not knowing one's own destructiveness, even as one is living it out in history.

Lies, it seems, can be characterized not just by their content, but by their function. Lies are not just attacks on linking. Lies stem from the inability to tolerate not knowing. In order to think and to know, our minds must be able to contain our experiences, letting new experiences in without being overwhelmed and reduced to chaos. For a brief moment we must know nothing at all (what Bion calls living without memory or desire), so that the container that is one's mind is open to new experience. Trouble is, this synapse between container and contained, this gap in time and space, can feel like an eternity – that is, like death. We must experience a little death in order to think and to know.[11] For many this experience is unbearable, for it recalls

---

[11] If this sounds cryptic, I can express the same thought in even more cryptic fashion by quoting that most original and recondite source, Bion (1984, 94). "Tolerance of doubt and tolerance of a sense of infinity are the essential connective in $\eth$n [an infinite recombination of thoughts] if K [knowledge] is to be possible." For Bion, linking is always about one thought, what he calls a preconception, holding another, a conception stimulated by an experience. In order to have experiences that change us, we must have this "tolerance of a sense of infinity," which I have reframed as an experience of a little death, a willingness not to know, and just for a moment not even to be. There are, as Bion's quote suggests, many ways to explain the same idea, even as there is something about Bion's mode of expression that tends to get lost in itself.

all too many little deaths in our lives – that is, too many failures of containment, what D. W. Winnicott (1965a) calls holding. Holding is the opposite of abandonment.

Attacks on linking destroy thought. Idealize the destruction of thought, and the result is contempt for thought, indeed the idealization of stupidity and mindlessness. Now we see why. Thought leads to self-transformation. The growth and development that comes from learning something new, coupled with the change in perspective that results, implies that one was previously incomplete, immature, unknowing in some way. If this possibility is itself unbearable, then not only will learning be impeded, but everything that is the opposite of learning and knowledge will be valorized. Strength, vitality, and self-certainty will be championed as sources of power. Doubt and reflection, including the doubt and reflection that create the gaps that allow one to learn something new, become merely signs of weakness and impuissance (Bion 1989, 89–99).

Herbert Rosenfeld (1988) writes about this process as if the Mafia had seduced the self. It is as though the death drive offers the self death-in-life in exchange for protection. Only instead of the Mafia, it sounds like Rosenfeld is writing about Satan. In either case the result is the same. Not only is the death drive directed at good objects outside the self, the sources of life, comfort, and support that Likierman writes of, but the death drive first comes to mimic, and then to attack the life affirming forces in the self, the forces that want to know and grow in truth and knowledge. By then it is too late. The life affirming forces have surrendered too quickly and completely to the Mafia, as only the destructive forces promise to be powerful enough to keep the dread of annihilation at bay. Søren Kierkegaard (1957, 38) called this dread (*angst*), "a presentiment of a something which is nothing," and that seems about right. Better to ally oneself with the devil than to be annihilated by nothingness.

Though this experience does not lend itself to words, we can try. Imagine that you suddenly recognize that in the scheme of things you know little, and that to learn even a little more you must die a little death (including the death of an idealized image of your own wisdom), a death that anticipates your own nothingness. Might you not be inclined – at least for a moment – to idealize your ignorance, even to call it a type of strength, say the strength of the simple and straightforward mind?

Perhaps the greatest contemporary image of the willful surrender to the tyranny of ignorance is George Orwell's *Nineteen Eighty-Four*. Indeed, we can now understand the meaning of that infamous slogan of Oceania, "Ignorance is Strength." Ignorance is strength because we need never admit doubt, weakness, uncertainty, or dependence on others for the help we need to grow in knowledge and understanding. *Nineteen Eighty-Four* is a great example for another reason as well: the distinction drawn between party members who enthusiastically shout the slogans, and the Inner Party members, men like O'Brien, who have become utterly cynical. For such men, there is only power and pain and privilege. O'Brien represents the death drive. Indeed, by the end of the book he has become death for Winston and Julia, torturing them until they are spiritually lifeless.

Though they are both destroyed, Winston and Julia know that the great enemy of the Inner Party, the death drive, is Eros, its only worthy opponent. "What overwhelmed Winston in that instant was admiration for the gesture with which Julia had thrown her clothes aside. With its grace and carelessness it seemed to annihilate a whole culture, a whole system of thought" (Orwell 1949, 29). Here is what Freud (1930) was so afraid of, and Herbert Marcuse (1966) so longed for, the hope behind *Eros and Civilization,* that Eros might overthrow a world.

Still a question remains: why does the attack on linking move so quickly from emotion to thought? Because the symbol and the object are originally one. The human body is originally equivalent to all the symbols that represent it, as the true story of torture reveals. Or as Janine Chasseguet-Smirgel (1994, 235) puts it, "symbol formation derives from the need of the child to protect his object, or parts of the object, from the effects of his attacks." Originally body and symbol were one. Emotional and intellectual development are inter-twined because intellectual development serves an emotional task: to protect the body of the beloved from one's hatred. If this development is stifled, thought will forever be cut off from its emotional roots. Good engineers, soldiers, professors, lawyers, doctors, dentists, accountants, and all the rest can emerge from such an experience (indeed, one might argue that the professions self-select for it), but their thought will be forever cut off at its nourishing source. Eichmann, who sometimes seemed as if he came from another planet, is only the extreme.

What would a society look like that failed to contain its members' unbearable emotions, and so encouraged attacks on linking? It need not be as extreme as the society that produced Eichmann, or O'Brien. Might it not look like a society that confused its citizens about good and bad, convincing them that this or that injustice is necessary to the smooth functioning of the productivity machine? Would it not, in other words, be a society that encouraged its members not to connect the dots – that is, not to make he links between the prosperity we enjoy, the existence of a permanent underclass in our society, as well as persistent poverty in the third world?

One could read the preceding paragraph as ideological cant. Read it instead in light of George Orwell's comments about the corruption of ordinary human decency by the corruption of language, be it the language of bureaucracy, doctrine, ideology, or academic life. Is it not the function of these languages to shatter the links between knowing and feeling? Anyone who is not corrupted by these languages, anyone who just looks and sees, will know, says Orwell, that kicking a coolie, procuring an abortion, abject and systematic poverty, and the destruction of natural beauty (to use four of Orwell's examples) are wrong.[12] Writing so clear that it seems to disappear, leaving only its subject, is the contribution intellectuals can make, perhaps their only contribution, to preventing doctrine, dogma, bureaucracy, laziness, and educated stupidity from getting in the way of ordinary human decency.

Trouble is, today we know, or think we know, that Orwell's windowpane theory of language, language so limpid it lets us see reality with nothing added or subtracted, is just one more rhetorical strategy, designed to create the illusion of objectivity, when it is of course the author who is creating the frame and form within which an infinitely interpretable reality is seen as objectively present to the reader.[13] While

---

[12] Orwell's four examples are (in order) from a newspaper column written in 1940, recalling his first experience of Asia in 1922; *Keep the Aspidistra Flying; The Road to Wigan Pier;* and *Coming Up For Air.*

[13] The windowpane theory of language is best expressed in Orwell's famous "Politics and the English Language" (1970a), originally published in 1946. For a fine discussion of the misleading character of the windowpane theory, see James Miller's "Is Bad

certainly true, this insight hardly matters. The key point is not the windowpane theory, but Orwell's moral particularism (Orwell, 1970b). They are related.

Study what is going on around you, pay attention to details, try to understand what they are, and how you stand in relationship to these details, empirically and morally. That is, make the links, preferably little links not big ones: not "globalization" (which at its worst links everything to everything else, which is functionally equivalent to linking everything to nothing), but how do I stand in relation to the person who cleans my house, serves my food, begs on the corner? There is no reason not to make larger, more encompassing theoretical links as well, but it is too easy to use big abstract links to dissolve little, concrete links, and so feel a little less: less responsible, less engaged – that is, just feel less. Theory too can obliterate the links between thought and feeling. Instead,

observe closely what's going on around you; pay attention to its particulars and try to understand why they are what they are; you will often know when something you see or have proposed to you is offensive to the natural order; when you know this, protest it, remove your cooperation from it, refuse to listen to those who offer theoretical justifications of it, and do what you can to prevent if from continuing. This won't, thinks Orwell, solve all political and economic problems. Some can only be addressed at the theoretical level. . . . [But] In the kinds of cases that interest him, Orwell thinks that the clear eye can be sure that what is recommended is wrong – surer than the intellect can be of the upshot of any theoretical argument at a high level of abstraction. This conviction lies at the heart of an Orwellian epistemology. (Griffiths 2004, 38)

This conviction also lies close to the heart of the natural law of reparation, which recognizes that it is not just big evils far away, but the evils of the average hating human heart, beginning with one's own, for which we must make reparation. But first we must see, and to see we must feel, and to feel we must repair the links that make knowing and feeling possible in the first place. That too is reparation. Since Plato, the image of knowing as seeing has been problematic, but unpacked in this way it makes sense: to see means to do the work, individual and social, that allows ordinary human decency to prevail.

Writing Necessary? George Orwell, Theodor Adorno, and the Politics of Language," in *Lingua Franca*, December/January, 2000.

My interviews have convinced me not so much that ordinary decency exists (I knew that), but that it exists in minimally coherent and thought-through form. For human decency to prevail, however, the links between knowing and feeling must be fostered, and this is best done, or at least begun, at the local level, about particulars. This is, I believe, how best to interpret Arendt when she writes that thinking may stand as a barrier to evil. Yes, but only when thinking is part of ordinary decent feeling.

Here, by the way, is the single most troubling possibility to come out of my interviews with informants: not what they said, but the metaphysical biology that characterized the way so many said it. I refer to informants' tendency to think about human equality not in terms of the metaphor of the human family, but in the more reductive, physical terms of "we all come from the same place," meaning we are all born, live, and die – there is nothing special about any of us. Attractive in some respects, it is now apparent that this way of thinking may be insufficiently symbolized, still stuck at that developmental level that tends to equate symbol with its physical object.

This troubling possibility would explain why informants are unable to use metaphysical biology as a metaphor that would allow them to tell a more complex story, such as the "family of man" story that explicates the UN Declaration of Human Rights. Metaphysical biology is truncated teleology because metaphysical biology does not symbolize anything larger than itself. Why? Because metaphysical biology it is not a fully developed symbol. No wonder it does not lend itself to further narrative development. Metaphysical biology is not really the material from which narratives are born, a symbolic representation of the real.

Elegant as this explanation is, it is not one in which I am particularly confident. Beyond all the obvious reasons, such as the small size of my sample, and the psychological and emotional subtlety of the issues involved, my primary reason is that I could discover no continuum among informants. Informants who thought in particularly reductive, biological ways about the relationship between nature and morality did not (as far as I could tell) hold to more truncated versions of the natural law than those who thought in less reductive, biological ways. The difference only appeared among the most imaginative, who thought in terms of the care perspective from the very beginning. An example may help to explain.

Leonard said "everyone is equal because everyone is born the same way, and dies the same way too."

What's that mean, I asked?

It means that you don't have a right to kill another person. Only nature can kill people.

Does that mean that you shouldn't hurt other people, because only nature can make people sick, or let a tree to fall on them or something? (Sometimes I got a little carried away with an informant's psycho-logic.)

"I never thought of it that way before; I'll have to think about it. But that sounds like a good idea."

Joann drew quite a different conclusion. "Nature is where we come from. But humans can improve on nature. That's what civilization is for. I mean, think about it: law, art, music – they all begin in nature, but humans make it better, so it [nature] fits our needs."

Actually, I don't know if Joann drew a different conclusion or not. What I know is that she thought about the relationship between nature and civilization, including morality, in a less reductive way. That, however, is not quite the same thing as saying she held a less truncated view of the natural law, or a more developed moral code than Leonard, for I do not believe she did, based on her answers to subsequent questions.

The relatively few informants who talked about nature in terms of the "human family," even if they did not use that term (two did), what I have called the care perspective, were different from the very beginning. As stated in the previous chapter, they tended to see the circumstances of human nature (I know of no substitute for this suspect term) as posing a terrible moral predicament: how to care for those whom one may never know and never even meet? Recall that this is not Carol Gilligan's care perspective. For Gilligan, care is always bound to a concern for particular others in particular circumstances. It is precisely the absence of both of these details that makes the moral position of these few informants so demanding. The imagination and identification necessary to think about anonymous others as part of the human family seemed especially challenging.

Thought, it turns out, has a great deal to do with the capacity for imaginative identification with others. The simplest task is to imagine that others are human beings who like me are born of woman, and who like me are destined to die. Almost every informant is capable of this, and so the question I will be addressing is not so much whether we can develop the care perspective in most informants (for I do not believe we can, at least not in this generation, and probably not in the next), but how far can the minimal natural law take us. Farther than one might expect, for embedded in the minimal natural law is a portion of care, the stirrings of *caritas*.

Xerxes (fifth century B.C.E), watching his army cross the Hellespont to invade Greece, pities the shortness of man's life, that so many will soon die. "No King," responds Artabanus, his uncle, "weep rather for this, that brief as life is there never yet was or will be a man who does not wish more than once to die rather than to live" (Herodotus, *Histories* 7.46). Here is our problem: how might reparation be cultivated so that it becomes thoughtful, imaginative pity for what we and others suffer in life, and not merely the distant, superior pity of the Persian King, who is sending tens of thousands to their deaths.

Few of us send anyone to their deaths, few of us would, but almost all of us who live well in the first world benefit from the suffering of others. How can we care for them? The first step, it turns out, is to be able to think about what one is doing by living every day. Orwell's moral particularism is an inspiration. So too is the less articulate struggle of several informants to figure out for themselves what it means to care for nameless others in an increasingly anonymous world.

Arendt's Failure

Though the judgment is harsh, one is forced to conclude that Arendt was unable to think deeply about evil, and that this is unfortunate. Not just because she rejects the idea that evil is "the manifestation of some unconscious malignancy," as McGowan puts it (1998, 31). Augustine rejects this too, and he still thinks deeply about evil, more deeply than his concepts should allow.

The superficiality of evil is an appearance, the result of what Bion calls attacks on linking, which prevents us from thinking about what we are doing. Arendt is not wrong to see that something like this was going on with Eichmann. Certainly she pays considerable attention to Eichmann's bizarre thought patterns, such as his inability to express himself except in clichés, what he called winged words (*geflügeltwörter*).

Where Arendt goes wrong is to take the phenomenon to be explained as though it were itself the explanation.

For Bion, the explanation is straightforward, if not simple: much of mental life is devoted to the destruction of thought, what he came to call the minus-K link (Bion 1989, 95–99). In other words, the death instinct operates at the level of thought itself. The result is utter irresponsibility, as we destroy the possibility of knowing what we are doing. For Bion, the defense mechanisms are really defenses against knowing reality. Emilia Steuerman puts the same point a little more abstractly when she states that the contribution of psychoanalysis to our understanding the evil of men like Eichmann "is the recognition that our capacity for thinking and tolerating separateness and differ- ence has to acknowledge an unconscious world that can attack the most basic links that make understanding possible" (Steuerman 2000, 35–36). Separateness and difference are, of course, leading categories in Arendt's political theory. Recognizing the reality of these categories is how humans express our love for the plurality of the world, above all the power of the world to surprise us with something new.

Arendt's failure to think deeply about evil is doubly ironic if one takes seriously the proposition that Augustine's concept of privation is the inspiration for the banality of evil. For Augustine is the world's first great theorist of inwardness, and it is this turn inward that Arendt for so long refused to make. While Augustine is the first great teacher of inwardness, his concept is not that of the *camera obscura*, in which my inwardness consists in my privileged access to my dark inner world. That view comes centuries later. Rather, Augustine thinks about inwardness much as the neo-Platonist Plotinus does. To turn inward is to find the presence of the divine mind already there. We each have our own inner worlds, but instead of a camera obscura, a better image is a room with no roof from which each of us, when we become sufficiently free of sin, is able to look up and see the same God. Inward- ness is not the same as isolation. One finds the clearest expression of Augustine's vision of inwardness when one puts together Augustine's account of neo-Platonism in book 7 of the *Confessions* with his account of memory in book 10.[14] Arendt's vision of thinking as an internal dia- logue, enriched by experiences in which one allows one's "imagination

[14] A lecture by Phillip Cary helped me understand this aspect of Augustine's teaching.

to go visiting," seems – like so much of her work – to originate in Augustine.

Toward the end of her life, Arendt did turn inward, suggesting that the Socratic dialogue was a dialogue one could as readily have with oneself as others.

> What Socrates discovered was that we can have intercourse with ourselves, as well as with others, and that the two kinds of intercourse are somehow related. Aristotle, speaking about friendship, remarked: "The friend is another self " – meaning that you can carry on the dialogue of thought with him just as well as with yourself. This is still in the Socratic tradition, except that Socrates would have said: The self, too, is a kind of friend. (Arendt 1978, pt 1, 188–189)

In this dialogue Arendt hoped to find an antidote to evil, as though thinking about what one was doing would itself prevent men and women from doing evil (Arendt 1978, pt 1, 180, 5). Perhaps it would, but one must first understand the way in which the malignancy of evil that Arendt rejects is first of all an attack on thought itself. About this Arendt had insight, but not one she was prepared to carry through.

"If there is anything in thinking that can prevent men from doing evil, it must be some property inherent in the activity itself, regardless of its objects" (Arendt 1978, part 1, p. 180; also p. 5). Why? So thought can reclaim a little something of the great spirit of Reason? Should we have no relationship with, no pity for, those whom we think about? And if Arendt believes that human relationships are unreliable as a moral guide, does that make thinking pure? Surely what Niebuhr (1988) says about Aquinas on reason goes double for Arendt on thinking. Thinking is far too implicated in self-deception, hubris, and arrogance, to ever be a reliable guide to ethics and morality. Thinking sounds a little too much like that grand and glorious Reason (*Vernuft*) that has so often gotten Western philosophy in trouble, as though reason could do anything on its own.

Not thinking, but reparation, the desire to make amends for all the hatred and envy one has felt toward the goodness in one's life, and in one's world, is the real alternative to evil. Reparation is love, the only force in the world powerful enough to overcome the *Todestrieb*, the worship of death and destruction. For Klein and Likierman, we long to destroy the good because it is good, and not me or mine. In other words, their perspective is strictly Satanic. (Unlike Satan, they do not endorse this perspective!) The perspective of Antigone is a little different. Dark Eros is the *Todestrieb* as *Liebestod*, Eros seeking its perfect fusion in death, rather than life. In either case, love is the only force strong enough to resist the utter willfulness of desire that would destroy what it cannot have or be, and this fits Antigone too.

Nothing else in the world comes close to the power of death and hate but love, which too often enters the scene after the damage has been done. Which is why love almost always takes the form of reparation, not preparation, so to speak. This, though, doesn't make thinking unimportant. On the contrary, thinking becomes even more important, for only thinking allows love to become responsible. Not the unimportance of thinking, but thinking's impotence as progenitor of loving action is my point.

Thought remains absolutely crucial to reparation because reparation is by its nature self-indulgent, indiscriminate. Left to him or herself, the evildoer (a category that includes us all) is as likely to choose painting a picture as an act of reparation over making reparation to those whom he or she has harmed. This harm may be indirect, even unavoidable, such as belonging to a wealthy society in a poor world. Only thinking can make reparation moral by directing reparation's passion toward those most truly in need, as well as by recognizing subtle connections (links), such as those between first world plenty and third world poverty. But only the impulse to make reparation can render thinking more than an exercise in reason. Thinking, it is apparent, is not merely an intellectual act. Thinking is the practice of intellectual responsibility; thinking means knowing what one is doing, and to whom one is doing it. It sounds simple but it's not.

From the perspective of reparative natural law, the prime principle "do good, avoid evil" possesses genuine empirical content. Evil is not just the privation (absence) of good, but the willful destruction of good because it is good. Evil is an expression of envy, the avatar of Thanatos. If we can do something as simple but hardly straightforward as protect the good from our own envy, hatred, and greed, then we shall have accomplished much indeed.

Foster life in all its aspects, from bearing children to building community, is the practical implication of "do good, avoid evil," according to Aquinas (ST, I–II, 91–96; II–II, 66). This is the leading implication of reparative natural law as well. Or as Julia Kristeva (2001, 84) puts it, "it is for Eros's sake that our anxiety about the annihilation of life penetrates the deepest layers of the psyche." We long to foster life in the face of death, but fear we are too hateful, envious, and weak. Building community in all its guises, from raising children to caring for the elderly, helps to gradually convince us that our love is stronger than our hate. Only then shall we be able to live within the depressive position, a place not as depressing as it sounds. Sobering would be a better term, as we come to know how much we hate as well as love. Living in the depressive position means living so as to let ourselves think about what we are doing, and to whom we are doing it. Only then can reparation become moral, and even then it's not so easy.

REPARATION IS NATURALLY SELFISH

Not the death drive, but the puzzling and mysterious quality of reparation is possibly the biggest, and certainly the most perplexing, barrier to transforming reparation into a decent foundation for the natural law. More precisely put, the barrier posed by the death drive is profound and relatively straightforward. The barrier to morality posed by reparation is profound and remarkably subtle.

While it often seems that Klein is writing about making reparation to other people, in many cases she is not. She is writing about making reparation to one's injured internal objects, which I shall simply define as the *ideas* one has about other people, and relationships generally. Klein generally calls these ideas objects. When these objects (ideas) come together to do things in one's mind, Klein refers to phantasies. My objection to Klein's way of putting it is not terminological. My objection is that Klein's formulation risks rendering reparation irresponsible – that is, all about me and my ideas. In other words, Klein risks turning morality into art.

That this aesthetic interpretation of Kleinian reparation is correct is seen in the work of Klein's followers, such as Hanna Segal, who write about art in the language of reparation, as though they were virtually the same thing. In "A Psycho-Analytical Approach to Aesthetics," Segal (1955, 397) writes that artistic creation requires that we mourn our lost objects; only when we do can we fully distinguish symbolic reality from its external counterpart. Only then can we get to work on internal reality, giving it beautiful form so as to compensate us for the loss of an external world, a loss that occurs not only through death, but through the separation of symbol and reality itself, a loss of identification with the object.

For Klein, the goal is to transform into symbols our phantasies of love and hate that otherwise remain so terribly embodied and reified. If Jesus Christ is the word (*logos*) made flesh (John 1:14), then Klein's goal is the opposite: to transform the phantasies of the flesh into the word, so that we might finally hear ourselves and be healed. Not only is this good therapy, but it is good natural law, promoting the ascendance of life over death, love over hate, good over evil. Rather than denying our pleasure in destruction, lest we destroy those we truly care for, we can acknowledge our sadism, and make reparation for it.

Only one thing gets lost in this scheme, the obligation to think about and make reparation to the ones truly harmed by our own and others' aggression. In the end, reparation is so inward-directed, so symbolically oriented that the injured other hardly matters to Klein. Reparation is symbolically oriented because the goal is to sever the body from the symbol, so that thought becomes freer, less reified (Klein 1975f). While it would be contrary to the telos of normal development to say that the ultimate goal should be to reconnect body and symbol, the goal should be to keep symbol and reality in constant conversation.

Consider the painter Ruth Kjär, who had been in a state of anguish since someone removed a painting from her wall. The empty space tormented her, as though it were her own empty body. Never having painted before, Kjär painted a "life size figure of a naked negress," as Klein puts it, demonstrating an extraordinary talent that she had never known she possessed. It is obvious, says Klein, "that the desire to make reparation, to make good the injury psychologically done to the mother, and also to restore herself was at the bottom of the com-pelling urge to paint" (Klein 1975e, 215–218). That the first image Kjär painted was of a naked negress is not addressed by Klein. Pre-sumably it was easier for Kjär to get in touch with her own feelings by projecting them into the sensual "primitive" other. Why this might not always be such a good idea is not addressed by Klein either.

In another account of reparation, Klein writes of reparation as an act of social contrition, as when "in former times . . . ruthless cruelty against native populations was displayed by people who not only explored, but conquered and colonized." And how might the colonists or their descendents make reparation? By "repopulating the country with people of their own nationality."

We can see that through the interest in exploring (whether or not aggression is openly shown) various impulses and emotions – aggression, feelings of guilt, love and the drive to reparation – can be transferred to another sphere, far away from the original person. Including far away from the original victims.(Klein 1964, 104–105)

Why is Klein so dense? One might argue that she wrote in less politically correct times, but that is hardly the whole reason. Consider Rustin's comment that "good object relations and reparation for past damage, in phantasy or reality, constitute a natural and desired condition of individuals" (1991, 35). Rustin makes this statement in an essay titled "A Socialist Consideration of Kleinian Psychoanalysis," in which he is concerned to demonstrate that Kleinian thought provides a resource for social democracy. But social democracy requires that people make reparation in reality, not just phantasy, and that they know the difference. With enough amendments, Klein's account can be made to support Rustin's good society, but it should be clear that for Klein it makes little difference whether the harm or the reparation stems from acts of phantasy or reality. It might, however, matter to the victims. (I never quite understood the desire of some African-Americans in the United States for reparations for slavery until I thought about it in the Kleinian sense of the term; now it makes perfect sense.)

Dozens of similar comments by Klein and her interpreters are readily found, all illustrating the way in which reparation in phantasy and reality are interchangeable. Consider Meltzer's comment that Richard, an early patient of Klein's, was able to repair "in phantasy, not in psychic reality," his good objects (Meltzer 1978, pt 2, 115). That's fine, as long as it is Richard as a ten-year-old boy in analysis we are concerned with, not Richard as a man sharing the world with others (Klein 1975b).

To be sure, Klein (1975d) distinguishes between genuine and manic or mock reparation, and one might be inclined to argue that only mock reparation substitutes reparation in phantasy for reparation in reality. But this is not what Klein says. Mock reparation is distinguished by its manic or pretend character – that is, the way it denies the harm inflicted, and the sadism behind it. Absent too is a genuine concern for the object. Like all manic defenses, manic or mock reparation is built upon an underlying phantasy of omnipotence: no one was really hurt, and if they were I can repair anyone or anything (Hinshelwood 1989, 340–342).

Trouble is, manic reparation is a way of characterizing the quality of the reparative phantasy, not the quality of the act. The distinction between manic and real reparation has little to do with whether I make reparation to a person whom I have harmed, or whether I go home and write a poem about it. Whether one authentically cares about the reality of the other distinguishes manic from real reparation, but because care is measured by phantasy and feeling, not action, the distinction is not morally useful.

In fact, the problem with Klein's account of reparation is a little more complex than this. Klein understands that getting reparation out into the world can create a good feedback loop, in which fostering life strengthens one's beliefs in one's own reparative powers. But, as with the colonialists, Klein gives us no reason to think that those we make reparation to should be those we have harmed. The Kleinian category of mock reparation, important as a warning against the tendency to deny the harm we have done with our hatred, is not very helpful here. Why? Why can't we say that repopulating a land decimated by explorers with the descendents of the explorers is mock reparation and manic denial? First, because Klein in no ways suggests it is. Second, and more importantly, what makes manic reparation manic is the denial of the hurt and pain inflicted, and especially the denial of the sadism behind it. Admit that, do something life enhancing about it, and all is forgiven, at least as far as one's internal world is concerned. Reparation recognizes pain and serves life, but it need not be the pain and life of the victims, or their descendents.

To end on this note would not be entirely fair, however. Nowhere in her work does Klein suggest that people think or feel about reparation the way I have just described. Never do people say to themselves, even unconsciously, "I'll paint a beautiful picture, and so feel less guilty about my rapacious greed." People do not, in other words, think like the popular media, which tells us that it's good to pray because it lowers one's blood pressure and strengthens the immune system.

On the contrary, Klein tells us over and over, no where more than in *Love, Hate and Reparation*, written for a popular audience, but in dozens of her works, that we love and make reparation to people because we care about them as people. When we are successful in doing so, we feel strengthened in the power of our love. Hope is reborn, the hope behind all hope: that love is stronger than hate, life stronger than death. Or as Albert Schweitzer (1965, 26) put it,

The essence of Goodness is: Preserve life, promote life, help life to achieve its highest destiny. The essence of Evil is: Destroy life, harm life, hamper the development of life. The fundamental principle of ethics, then, is reverence for life.

None of my criticisms of Klein's concept of reparation should obscure the fact that about the basics Klein got it right.

The tendency to aestheticize reparation is a quality of Klein's theoretical account of the world of internal objects. It is not reflected in her writings about the lives of real people. It is as though the internal world of relations among ideas we have of people lives a life parallel to that of the real world of human relations. They interact, but each is only intermittently in contact with the other. Or as Meltzer (1978, pt 2, 44–46) puts it, "reparation began to take on a more mysterious meaning" in Klein's later work. "The true reparation is something that happens when the mental condition, the mental atmosphere is conducive to the objects repairing one another." This seems about right, and oddly mysterious indeed.

How to think about the tendency to make reparation primarily an internal drama, in which objects destroy and repair each other according to their own script, one that only loosely glosses the real world? I suggest we think about it as Aquinas did about the German robbers, among whom according to Julius Caesar theft was considered good (ST I–II, 94, 4, 6). Brought up to admire theft as noble self-assertion, the German robbers never learned any differently. Similarly, those who would make reparation for the native peoples they have destroyed by colonizing the new land with their own kind have never truly learned the difference between self and other, between reparation as mere feeling and reparation as an ethic that asks us to think about what we have done and to whom we have done it.

The result is immorality, but the failure is as much intellectual as moral. If, that is, we understand intellectual as Bion does, as a failure of thinking as linking. The reparative impulse is present, but it requires education and cultivation so that it is directed toward the right people. Or, to paraphrase Aristotle (*N Ethics* 1109a25–30), it's easy to make reparation. Difficult is to make the right amount of reparation to the right people in the right circumstances. Because it is difficult, doing so is a rare, fine and laudable achievement, one fostered by education in all its aspects, from a good upbringing to a good society. If it is properly cultivated, we may say that the passion of reparation becomes a virtue – that is a civilized human excellence, what Aquinas called *misericordia,* what I shall call pity. That is the topic of the next chapter.

4

Making Reparation Moral

The contemporary connotations of the term "pity" could be misleading. The phrase "I pity you" is today often little more than an insult. Nevertheless, I will use the English translation, rather than the more elegant Latin original (*misericordia*) precisely in order to avoid the elegance of a Latin term, at least for English readers. For Aquinas, pity is not just a sloppy sentiment. Pity may be cultivated in the same way that all the other virtues are cultivated, by living in a community that teaches and practices them (ST II–II, 30, 3). The transformation of pity into a virtue marks a subtle but profound difference between Aquinas' *Summa Theologica* and Aristotle's *Ethics*. About the virtues of everyday life, one expects these two authors to reach similar conclusions. Certainly this is Veatch's position (2005). However, if one looks closely one finds a delicate but radical difference between them.

Pity is grief or sorrow over someone else's distress, says Aquinas, precisely insofar as one understands the other's distress as virtually identical to one's own. "Among the virtues that relate us to our neighbor *misericordia* is the greatest" (ST II–II, 30, 4).[1] Particularly significant is what it takes to feel pity. Not just noblesse oblige or mercy, but that another's suffering could be one's own because one is a vulnerable human living among other humans who are similarly vulnerable. Not

---

[1] I follow MacIntyre's (1999) argument in *Dependent Rational Animals* closely at points, diverging from it at others. Mostly I am inspired by it, even as I believe that we are dependent every day of our lives, not just when young, old, or infirm.

only that, but shared vulnerability is what binds a human community, in the sense that at any moment any one of us could become weak and needy; if we live long enough all of us will.

Curiously, this way of thinking is not alien to the informants interviewed for Chapter 2. On the contrary, it is this sense of shared vulnerability, expressed as a sense of shared mortality, that is the foundation of the minimal natural law. In other words, much of what informants said about the natural law, while not an expression of misericordia, did contain the necessary elements of that emotion, as when Ned said "Everyone is equal because everyone gets hurt so easily. I don't mean just physically, but mentally, emotionally. That's why we have laws. But we need more than laws, we need, you know . . . what my great aunt used to call good manners." (I did not, by the way, classify Ned as among the few who represented the "care perspective," for he did not go on to develop the theme.) For a number of informants, it would not be misleading to state that the minimal natural law, truncated as it is, stands in a not too distant relationship to pity. It's not supposed to work that way; for most Americans, pity is a virtual term of contempt, but reality among informants is more complex.

Why didn't Aristotle get it? Why was Aristotle as contemptuous of pity as the average American is supposed to be? It's a puzzle, especially since pity was not an alien virtue to the Greeks, or even to Aristotle (*Poetics*, c 6). As W. B. Stanford (1983, 154) puts it, "the supreme tragic emotion, to judge from the surviving tragedies, is *eleos* or *oiktos*. Both words are generally translated into English as pity." With the phrase "supreme tragic emotion," Stanford means something like "looked upon with the greatest awe and respect." Aristotle doesn't get it because to see pity as a virtue means to understand everybody, including oneself, as dependent, vulnerable, bound to others in a web of need. Everything one has or is becomes gift. Though Aristotle, as did all the Greeks, certainly understood the caprice of life, what is called *tuche*, best translated not as luck or fate, but as contingency, everything that happens to a man or woman, Aristotle did not know how to embrace *tuche* – that is, how to make it holy.

Instead of pity, Aristotle posited the virtue of *megalopsychos*, the characteristic virtue of the big-souled man, potent enough to confer benefits, sufficiently superior so that he never need receive them (*N. Ethics*, 1124b 9–10). Or as MacIntyre (1999) puts it,

We recognize here an illusion of self-sufficiency, an illusion apparently shared
by Aristotle, that is all too characteristic of the rich and powerful in many times
and places, an illusion that plays its part in excluding them from certain types
of communal relationships. (127)

MacIntyre refers to relationships built upon acknowledged dependence, a fleshy human web of mutual need. Only in communities
of mutual need can the care we extend toward others stem from a
genuine identification with their suffering, what is called pity or compassion. Recall, by contrast, the key characteristic of mock or manic
reparation: that it is built upon the illusion of omnipotence, that I
could never really and truly need someone else in the same way that
I need air to breathe and food to eat. The ability to make genuine
reparation, it seems, depends upon the ability to feel vulnerable, in
need of pity.

Overcoming this blind spot took another tradition, one centered
in Jerusalem, not Athens. No one combined the traditions so as to
preserve a roughly Aristotelian way of thinking about the virtues with
a transformation of their content so as to include pity (*misericordia*)
better than Aquinas. Put more precisely, Aquinas understood the illu-
sions about human autonomy one must abandon in order to make
pity a virtue – not just a sentiment, but a way of life.

Or at least this is a standard reading. In fact, we need not travel to
Jerusalem to discover this insight. It can already be found in Athens:
not in the writings of her philosophers, but in the collective cele-
brations that were her tragedies. Jean-Pierre Vernant defines Greek
tragedy as the heroic values of myth subject to the perspective of the
democratic citizen (Vernant and Vidal-Naquet 1988, 26). Tragedy is
born when men become convinced that they can act more nobly than
the gods: not because humans can compete with gods, but because
humans can offer what the gods never can: pity and compassion. Where
Plato would make *sophrosune*, or rational self-control, the measure of
nobility, the tragic poets would make pity and compassion nobility's
standard.

One of several reasons Antigone would bury her brother is simply out of pity for his naked humiliation in death (28–32, 422–426).
Amphitryon, father of the suffering Heracles, says to Zeus, "I, mere
man, am nobler [have more *arête*] than you, great god" (Euripides,

Heracles, 342). This is not mere hubris talking, but fact; Amphitryon is capable of depths of pity and compassion than Zeus can hardly imagine.

This does not, of course, equip man to compete with the gods – that would be hubris indeed. Rather, Amphitryon's humane assurance allows men to think of the polis as a place where they may offer each other support, pity, and compassion in the face of the depredations of the gods and the harshness of life in general. J. Peter Euben's comments on the puzzling resolution of Aeschylus' *Oresteia* capture this ideal well. The *Oresteia* does not end suffering but collectivizes it through the medium of dramatic performance (1990, 90).

As *Oedipus Tyrannus* is Freud's signature tragedy, so the *Oresteia* is Melanie Klein's (1975g), as discussed briefly in Chapter 1. While Klein does not address the social dimension of tragedy at Athens, she understands that the *Oresteia* is not just about the return to mental health of Orestes after being ordered by Apollo to kill his mother, Clytemnestra. The trilogy is concerned with more than the movement of an individual from the paranoid-schizoid to the depressive position. Rather, the *Oresteia* is concerned with how an entire community comes to deal with its Furies, these primitive, blood-sucking representatives of pure talion morality. Not only by literally placing the Furies under law and justice (in the grand finale the Furies are escorted beneath the Areopagus, where the first Athenian law courts were said to meet), but also by placing the Furies under the persuasive powers of Athena. Here Athena represents not rational argument (her arguments are as bad as Apollo's), but the ability to contain the Furies' rage, so that they, and we, might feel pity for Athens (Alford 1990).

Trouble is, if we assume (correctly) that it was originally Athenians watching the play, then there is a self-referential quality to the pity, otherwise known as self-pity, which is why thought, thinking as linking, remains so important. Even, or especially, the virtue of pity may become self-indulgent. In this regard, pity is not automatically the best counterweight to the self-indulgence of reparation. Pity need not become self-pity; nothing in Aquinas or the Greek tragedians suggests it must. Indeed, without some self-pity, pity for others is likely impossible, for in pity we echo another's pain. But the self-indulgence of pity remains a risk. As Hannah Arendt points out, one of the tricks of Heinrich Himmler was to transform the "animal pity" of the Nazi killers for their victims into self-pity, so that instead of saying

What horrible things I did to people!, the murderers would be able to say: What horrible things I had to watch in the pursuance of my duties, how heavily the task weighed upon my shoulders. (Arendt 1965, 106)

It is the task of thought to remain aware of this evidentially natural tendency to pervert pity.

To collectivize suffering is a key dimension of pity, what humans can do for each other that the gods cannot. Tragedy not only describes this shared suffering; it *is* this shared suffering. Greek tragedy celebrates the willingness and ability of the citizens of Athens to share each others' pain. It is to this aspect of Athens' greatness that the realist Thucydides refers when praising the noble city (*History*, 2.60). Like the tragic poets, Pericles transforms pain sharing into an act of nobility.

One is inclined to argue that Greek pity, with its almost physical fusion with the suffering other is not the same as the *misericordia* of Aquinas. As Neoptolemus says to Philoctetes, "I have been in pain for you: I have been in sorrow for your pain" (Sophocles, *Philoctetes*, 805). But pity as virtual fusion with the pain of the suffering one is hardly a concept alien to Christian thought. About eleos and oiktos, Stanford says

there is no question here of the pitier being separate from another's agony. You respond to it in the depths of your being, as a harp-string responds by sympathetic resonance to a note from another source. . . . The same depth of physical feeling is expressed in the Greek versions of the Bible by a verb that indicates a sensation in one's entrails (*splanchnizo*), and in the phrase in 1 John 3, 17, translated in the Authorised Version as "bowels of compassion." (Stanford 1983, 156)

A CULTURE OF CONTAINMENT

As a complete virtue, pity is reparation plus thought, thinking as linking. Pity is reparation that takes responsibility for what it means to live in the world, not just in the cave of one's mind. Pity is not, however, merely an individual achievement. If reparation is natural (albeit naturally selfish), thinking as linking is unnatural, at least as an individual achievement. Thinking as linking requires the provision of containment. In other words, Freud (1930, 65) was wrong to reassure his friend that we cannot fall out of this world. We can, for today, at least in the United States (and not just in the United States), there is little in the way of a social safety net to catch us. With the term "social safety net" I include a society's social welfare programs, but also its sense of community, spiritual, and family life, including its sense of and place for extended family – that is, the generations that span the life span, and so make our existence more real, by personifying where life begins and ends. A social safety net refers to all the institutions that help contain our unbearable feelings of dread (*angst*). As good a definition as any of what it means to fear falling out of this world. Only when this unbearable anxiety is contained is thinking as linking possible. Otherwise, we defend ourselves via attacks on linking, with the result that we never let ourselves know what we feel. Even worse, we become the antithought police, devaluing thought itself.

In putting it this way I have moved some distance from Klein, though how far is difficult to determine. One might argue that Kleinian thinking finds its social analog in individualism, but that would not be correct either. Not individualism, but the cloistered or monastic self, which longs to remain secluded with its internal objects, its ideas of others, prevents reparation from becoming pity. This is what Kristeva (2001, 237) means when she says that "all that Melanie demands from the powers originating from the outside is that they exist as little as possible, that they do not encroach too much upon the adjustments made by internal objects bouncing between envy and gratitude." From Kristeva's perspective, people just want to be left alone so they can make reparation to their internal objects. Kristeva's judgment is harsh, but not unfair, capturing the limit in Klein's thought, the way in which reparation is related to real others, but reluctant to leave the cave of the mind, that telluric place where Antigone communed with the natural law, all mixed up with Thanatos and nonbeing.

Does this mean that Rustin's account of Klein as virtually a theorist of social democracy is wrong? No, the social, moral, and teleological dimensions of Klein's work are real, coexisting (if not comfortably) with the cloistered self, at home with its objects. Bion's contribution is to show us that the way out of the cave of the mind (that is, how we might make contact with reality, always Bion's chief concern) is at the same time the pathway to moral responsibility.

For reparation to become Eros, the healing force that holds this broken world together (Plato, *Symposium* 202e–203a), reparation must become social, more akin to the misericordia of Aquinas. But then it is no longer reparation in the Kleinian sense, the reader might reply.

True enough, for now reparation is combined with thinking about what we are doing, the reparative impulse coupled with the moral and intellectual courage to make the links between feeling, acting, and our responsibilities to those upon whom our acts have fallen, as well as an appreciation of our own terrible vulnerability once we have left the cave of our minds and entered into this world.

One more distinction must be made. Society's greed and aggression is not necessarily my own. Nevertheless, I live in this society, and share its benefits. The first task of an ethical society is to help its members connect the dots, pointing out, for example, the connections between the prosperity I enjoy, the existence of an underclass in my society, as well as persistent poverty in the third world. That too is thinking as linking, as I have argued. At a more personal level, I cannot always make reparation to the victims of my own aggression. Some have died, moved on, and so forth. It is the task of an ethical culture to contain emotional intruders, feelings so strong they threaten to shatter the self, while directing our reparation toward those most deserving: some combination of those whom I have actually harmed and their symbolic stand-ins, the widow, the orphan, the afflicted, and the destitute (Psalms 82:3–4; II Esdras 2:20–22). Such a culture makes it possible for us to think about what we are doing, and to act on this basis.

The novelist and philosopher Iris Murdoch (1998, 70) characterizes natural law morality as one in which "the individual is seen as held in a framework which transcends him." With the term "transcend" Murdoch refers not necessarily to a cosmological design, but a framework as big as the human world. Those familiar with the work of D. W. Winnicott (1971), an independent-minded student of Klein, will know that one can read the term "held in a framework which transcends him" in a different way. For Winnicott, feeling securely held is the condition of transitional experience, as he calls it, in which we let ourselves belong to the experience. If we are securely held, we do not have to worry about falling out of the world. We don't even have to think about it. We can just be. Mothers are generally the first ones to hold us, but holding isn't just for babies. Culture and the meanings it provides are leading ways adults are held.

Culture would mean nothing if it were merely outside of me, an alien thing. But only crazy people live entirely in their own private cultures. Culture is what Winnicott calls a transitional object, me and not me at the same time, a shared experience. Holding is (for our purposes) a synonym for what Bion calls containment, the sense that others, not just other people, but the stories a culture tells its members, make sufficient sense of dangerous and dreadful emotions so that they need not overcome us with dread. Absent the feeling of being held or contained, these emotions threaten to tear us to pieces, so that there is no safe place to call home, and no person called "me" left to go there. Greek tragedy is containment, or holding, though we would do well to remember that the original experience of Greek tragedy was very unlike that of today's experience of reading a play, indeed, very unlike going to the theater.[2]

Those narratives known as natural law should be judged not only by whether they are true or false (if we are truly being held, we do not always need to ask), but by whether they avoid crushing us with their rigidity, or dropping us in their vacuity. Jacques Maritain writes of our knowledge of the natural law as developing "within the double protecting tissue of human inclinations and human society" (Maritain 2001, 35–36). Maritain understands the way in which culture is not just second nature, but a second skin, woven together with our own. It is this that makes culture the transitional object par excellence.

Why is holding so important? For all the reasons Bion points out in his study of attacks on thinking as linking. Only if we are properly held, our anxieties framed and formed by the experiences of another capable of containing them for us, can we afford to think about what we are doing, and to whom we are doing it. At first the one who holds us must be a person. Later the container may become more symbolic: a

---

[2] Before the tragedies were presented at the festival known as the Great (or City) Dionysia, the names of those men who had benefited Athens in some way were read out in front of the audience, and the honors that had been bestowed upon them were listed. Subsequently, the male war orphans were paraded upon the stage, partly in order to demonstrate the degree to which the Athenians regarded their bodies as the city's own, partly to demonstrate the generosity of the city in supporting the orphans until their eighteenth birthdays, when they too would turn their bodies over to the state, while keeping their minds for themselves. Or so says Thucydides (*History*, I.70). Likely a casualty list was also read (Winkler and Zeitlin 1990). These and half a dozen other civic ceremonies remind us that the presentation of the tragedies was nothing like "going to the theater." Rather, it was an opportunity for the (male) polis to assert itself as an enterprise of war and conquest, not as close knit perhaps as the Spartans, though perhaps it would be more accurate to simply to say more imaginatively knit, through a life of ritual rather than life in barracks.

God, a tradition, an ideal worth living for. Only if we are properly held or contained does morality become possible. Otherwise thinking is just too terrifying, the emotions thinking evokes too alien, intrusive, and shattering. And so we destroy the links that make thought, including moral thought, possible. "Ignorance is Strength."

To feel what one is feeling, to experience one's terrible vulnerability to emotion, indeed one's dreadful exposure to life and death, is no easy matter. Nor is it easy to take responsibility for one's acts of omission and commission. At least as difficult is taking some (not all) responsibility for the failures of one's society, while making reparation to those most in need. To know and do all this is no easy matter, and yet all this and more is required if reparation is to become moral. *When I refer to reparative natural law it is this combination of reparation and thinking that I have in mind, a combination called the cultivation of pity.*

The reparative natural law is itself a dimension of this experience of being held. Like Thomistic natural law properly understood (or perhaps I should just say like Thomistic natural law as it is understood by Maritain), reparative natural law is a narrative, a story that like all stories is fully understood only in terms of its end. Only when we know how the story turns out do we understand it; only then does the story have meaning. We cannot know this about our own lives until they are almost over, and perhaps not even then. This is, of course, the meaning of the ancient Greek proverb, "call no man happy before he is dead" (*Oedipus the King*, 1529–1530). We can, however, know the teleological or developmental ideal of reparative natural law as an account of an ideal life into whose pattern we can try to fit our own. In this regard, reparative natural law is itself a narrative that holds us, a tissue to wrap around us as though it were a second nature, a second skin. This, though, is not enough. The symbolic, narrative holding of the natural law must be accompanied by the less symbolic, more real holding of the social safety net, communities, and families. Or rather, all these symbolic realities (some are just closer to the body, indeed to the life of the body, than others) must work together. Holding is being cared for, with sufficient subtlety that one does not always have to ask or even know.

If one were to put reparative natural law in the form of a postulate or statement, it might read like this (even if it is a little long winded).

You ought to make reparation to those you have harmed in reality, as well as to their real-world stand-ins, the needy, the desperate, and the despised. Making reparation ought to become your life's work, for in all the ways that you may make reparation, from making love, to raising children, to supporting yourself and your family, to caring for your community, to protecting and promoting the values of your society, you are doing the work of Eros, and so keeping Thanatos at bay, both in your own life, and that of your society. Of course, you may also make reparation by acts of individual creativity, but you should remember that the world for which you are morally responsible does not begin and end at the door of your studio or study, far less at the entrance to the cave of your mind.

If you are fortunate, which means morally well-educated and blessed with at least a modicum of talent, the social and the creative dimensions of reparation will reinforce each other. As you paint a beautiful picture of a naked negress (to recur to Klein's image), you may be reminded not only of your white relatives whom you have hated as well as loved, but of African-Americans and others whom many of us have used to hold alienated parts of ourselves. This is more likely when society and culture encourage us to think about what we are doing, rather than being organized around denial and projective identification, as societies and cultures usually are.

Why can't I just stay home and make reparation to my internal objects? Rustin has given part of the answer. As the self is inherently social and relational, so is reparation. The other, and more important, part of the answer is that doing so is a lie. Thinking means linking. Thinking means saying what we are doing, with some sense of the feeling and phantasy behind it, such as sadism, envy, love, and hate. Thinking as linking is a developmental telos that is constantly endangered by all the enemies of good development, above all failed containment, what Winnicott calls holding. Containment begins with family, and comes to include all of a decent society, from its art and literature to its police and welfare programs, to its retirement security. Containment is what keeps our natural paranoid-schizoid impulses from concluding that the world, including the world of our own uncontained emotions, is out to destroy us. The adult version of containment is a combination of loving personal relationships and a decent social compact. Cultural containment is provision of the support necessary for reparation and thought to talk with each other, and with the world.

For centuries natural law was central to Western culture, indeed to the very being of a majority of Western men and women. The question today is not how can we make natural law central again, for that is likely impossible. My research with young people supports that conclusion, while at the same time showing that the core of natural law remains, a plot outline I have called it. The question is how we might fill in this outline, and whether a roughly Kleinian interpretation would be helpful: either to those who work with young people, or to the young themselves. I return to this question in the conclusion of this chapter, though I admit I have no answers, only more questions. MacIntyre has answers, and his answer in *After Virtue* is by now notorious. A few men and women of good will may retreat into their own small communities in order to survive the new dark ages (1981, 244–245). Surely these communities will hold their members tightly, but if they hold them too tightly, they will crush the life from them.

For now it must suffice to note the continuity between reparative natural law and the traditional natural law.

1. Natural law is rooted in nature. For Aquinas (ST I–I 79, 12), like Augustine, natural law originates in a direct experience of the goodness of nature. For reparative natural law, natural law is rooted in the experience of hating those we love, an experience that leads to guilt, and a strong desire make reparation to those we love. Doing so restores an original experience of the goodness of nature in which we can share, but need not devour.

2. The desire to make reparation is strong, but left untutored it is likely to be expressed in sentimental and selfish ways. The tutoring required is not intellectual, but social, though a close reading of what Aquinas means by "shun ignorance" suggests that this is already a false dichotomy (ST I–II, 92, 2). Living in decent communities one learns to cultivate pity. One is able to do so because one feels contained by a fleshy human web of relationships, allowing one to think and feel at the same time. Aquinas and Maritain both assume the existence of such communities as a condition of the natural law. For similar reasons, MacIntyre (1999) argues that neither in the family nor in the nation, but only in community, can the virtues of acknowledged dependence be practiced. In the family, acknowledged dependence

is not so much a virtue as a way of life (MacIntyre thinks of dependence in terms of infancy, sickness, and old age; other dimensions of dependence elude him). In the nation, not pity but justice is the reigning virtue.

3. Reparation is an experience of binding moral obligation, based on the guilt of having hated and harmed (at least in one's imagination, and often in reality) those whom one loves and cares for. For children, parents are the most likely targets of reparation. For adults, the widow, the orphan, and the stranger are the traditional Biblical stand-ins. Just open your eyes and look around, and you will see the victims of hate and greed everywhere. Being an adult means making reparation not just for one's own transgressions, but for the transgressions of all the groups to which one belongs, including one's nation and, indeed, the human race. Why this obligation is experienced as binding – that is, the way in which reparative natural law, like the traditional natural law, binds nature and moral obligation, is discussed in the last section of this chapter.

THE OPPOSITE OF NIHILISM

Here is a good place to return to the interviews, in order to explain a puzzling phenomenon that seems best understood in terms of the absence of a culture of containment. For better or worse this includes the irrelevance of those small communities of virtue to which MacIntyre refers. Informants live unsheltered in a cosmopolis of contending economic and social forces, and they know it.

Almost half of all informants seemed secretly, even ashamedly, to believe in God. To be sure, the presence of secret belief likely has much to do with academic and contemporary culture, particularly in the northeastern United States. But it also has to do, I suspect, with the fact that secrets are most powerful when they are held close to the heart. To talk out loud about God in this secular world is already to have begun losing Him. Or so it seemed to me that this is what many informants believe.[3]

---

[3] Because issues such as private religion are involved, what Bellah et al. (1985) call "Sheilaism," after a woman who named her religion after herself, standard surveys of religious belief are especially suspect. "Especially," because almost every survey

Tom put it as clearly as any when he said in response to my pushing him on the question "Why be moral?"

"I believe in God. But I know that I can't say that here, that you wouldn't accept it as an answer."

How do you know, I asked? I might believe in God too.

"Because this is a public school [a public university actually]. We live in a culture where everyone has such different beliefs that it's better just to keep these things to oneself."

Do you go to religious services, I asked?

Tom smiled sheepishly, and that was that.

Not every informant who said something like "in a secular society, God is not a convincing enough answer to the question why be moral" seemed to secretly believe in God. But it was my strong impression that almost half the informants did. Comments such as "I could refer to God, but at the university it's better to talk in terms of law and contracts," were not uncommon, and are the source of my hypothesis.

One way Nietzsche (1974) writes about nihilism is as though it were atheism with a bad conscience (*Gay Science*, sections 125, 346). People live as though God no longer exists, but they are not willing to say this, even to themselves, for to do so would be to fall into an abyss of absolute moral freedom. The semisecret belief in God of many informants is not only not nihilism, but in many ways its opposite, a phenomenon

of religion in the United States is subject to what is called demand performance pressure: people tend to say to strangers what they think they ought to say. Thus, standard surveys of religious identification and participation are not a trustworthy source of comparison. Consider the American Religious Identification Survey, a telephone survey of about 50,000 people in forty-eight states, conducted in 2001. ("American Religious Identification Survey," by The Graduate Center of the City University of New York, at: http://www.gc.cuny.edu/studies/.) For a methodological critique see www.religioustolerance.org/chr_prac2.htm.

General Point of View: Religious or Secular?

Outlook	All Adults	Young (18–34)	Senior (over 64)
Religious	37%	27%	47%
Somewhat religious	38	43	34
Somewhat secular	6	9	3
Secular	10	14	7
Don't know/refused	9	7	9

for which we do not yet have a name. Acting and talking as though they don't believe, many seem to harbor not secret doubts, but secret beliefs, not always of the conventional religious variety.

What I could not determine is how informants' sub rosa belief in God affected their views on morality. Since there seemed to be slightly more underground believers among the metaphysical biologists, it may be that when they say things like "we all come from the same place, so that means we're all equal," the abyss between is and ought is bridged by God. Yet, even as I write this I am not convinced. The bridge theory attributes more theological and philosophical angst to informants than seems warranted. Since most don't worry about the naturalistic fallacy in the first place, they don't need a clandestine *deus ex machina* to hold is and ought together.

People are not required to profess their religious beliefs, certainly not to an interviewer. The trouble with the way many informants seem to believe in God is that it makes Him unavailable as a resource or refuge when the minimal natural law provides insufficient guidance or support. In this regard informants are in precisely the position that H. L. A. Hart would put them in, where stepping outside the natural law means stepping into a no man's land where there is nothing to be said, only a decision to be made. To be sure, Hart is referring to stepping outside the positive law, whereas I am referring to stepping beyond the minimal natural law, but the situation is identical for informants. To step beyond the bounds of the law requires the type of guidance and support that community and tradition, including religious tradition, provide. The natural law is both.

One might argue that I invoke religion in the spirit of Alexis de Tocqueville (2000, 502–506), who was little concerned with the existence of God, and greatly concerned that people believe in God. Not just so that they would be less greedy, but so that they would be comforted in their isolation and loneliness in a New World, where every link to past and place has been sundered. Otherwise, people are likely to cling to the group, even as they call it freedom. "Individualism" is the term Tocqueville came up with to explain this strange new phenomenon, each isolated individual thinking the same thoughts while calling them his own. As though unacknowledged and unrecognized conformity in thought could substitute for the broken bonds of tradition and community.

Though I would take it as compliment to be told that I write about religion in the spirit of Tocqueville, I'm not sure I do. I write about religion as a narrative that once gave natural law its resonance. Not its logical possibility, the warrant we need to proceed from is to ought. Religion only provides that for those who believe in religion in the first place, and that's cheating as far as the naturalistic fallacy is concerned. What religion provided was the story behind the story, the not so hidden content that gave the minimal natural law its depth. Here I must disagree with the man who inspired me, Henry Veatch (2005), who argues as if an Aristotelian version of the natural law could stand on its own. Perhaps, but we have seen how truncated that version has become. Veatch makes the good point that as the teleological basis for natural law has withered and become improbable, natural law comes in fact (though not necessarily in admitted fact) to depend more upon God, as no other grounds remain, despite all the clever reasoners from Kant to Gewirth (1978) to T. M. Scanlon (1998) and the flying uranium spewer.

But is not Veatch drawing the distinction between God and Aristotle too sharply? As part of the UNESCO philosophers' effort to justify the UN Declaration, they sent out a questionnaire to leading intellectuals, including Mohandas Gandhi, Pierre Teilhard de Chardin, Benedetto Croce, and Aldous Huxley! Most replied. Though the differences among these men were substantial, their beliefs were not private in anything like the sense of informants' private religion. On the contrary, all had their own philosophies, embedded in distinct yet overlapping cultures and worldviews. As Maritain tells us, although these men differed greatly in their reasoning, all agreed that the UN Declaration spoke to a higher truth (Glendon 2001, 76–78). Might we not locate each of their conclusions somewhere between a traditional view of God and Aristotle? To be sure, we could get to this higher truth more directly through a traditional view of God or Aristotle, but philosophy is not lapidarian for its own sake.

Private religion, religion held secretly (except in such places where religion is persecuted, which is an entirely different matter) lacks depth and resonance. Called upon as a source of moral support, it melts like butter in the sun. Not just because private religions lacks social support, though it does. But because private religion is likely to possess qualities of fantasy, God a secret helper or some such, and these fantasies do not live long when exposed to reality. At least this was my impression after talking with several informants, but about this finding I am not confident. Or rather, I remain puzzled. The phenomenon of private religion exists; what it means I am not certain.

Robert Bellah (1985) and his associates found the phenomenon of private religion in their study of the isolated American who wants to give him or herself to something larger, but lacks the narrative resources by which to make sense of his or her longings. The authors of *Habits of the Heart,* even gave private religion a name. "Sheilaism" they called it, after a woman who named her religion after herself. But, while private religion exists, and its implications are seemingly more disturbing than reassuring, beyond this it is difficult to say. Like the minimal natural law, one finds the living body of what one thought had fallen into desuetude, but some of the animation is missing.

MARITAIN AND BRITISH OBJECT RELATIONS THEORY

For some time now I have been writing as though Thomistic natural law, as interpreted by Jacques Maritain, readily blends into the natural law of reparation, as represented by Klein. Can it be that simple? Must I not do intellectual damage to one or the other, or both, in order to compare a virtual Catholic brother (though Jacques and Raïssa were married, evidently they practiced celibacy) with a rather flashy, culturally Jewish woman psychoanalyst? No, and the reason is simple: Klein's categories are essentially religious: original sin, trespass, guilt, and salvation through reparation.

Original sin is the child's hatred of the mother, the source of all goodness. More than this, the child wishes to destroy this goodness, even at the cost of his or her own mental life.

Trespass is the desire to desire to take all for oneself, leaving nothing for others, not even for the one who gives so generously of her food, her time, her love. It is in this regard that Klein writes in terms of the young child's desire to scoop out the mother's body and with it all the good it contains, leaving behind an empty husk.

Guilt arises at almost the same time as sin and trespass, as the young child comes to recognize that he or she loves and cares for the one he or she would so recklessly exploit and destroy out of greed and envy.

Salvation through reparation allows the young child – indeed it allows us all – to make recompense for our sins, providing a way to care and repair the ones we love, the same ones we would have ravaged. Reparation allows us to do this to particular loved ones we have harmed or wished to harm, as well as their real world stand-ins, the pitiful, the pathetic, and the despised, wherever they are found.

But perhaps these parallels are not the most important implicit religious elements in Klein's thought. Intellectual parallels are the creation of scholars. More important is the fact that the love that Klein writes about is not the Eros that has inhabited philosophy and psychology from Plato to Freud. The love that Klein writes about can only be called *caritas*, a term that Klein herself does not use. Defined as affection, love, or esteem, the term connotes the value of the object loved rather than the intensity of desire. In other words, caritas is distinct from Eros, which as everyone from Plato to Freud knows retains at its core a selfish element. Socrates' mythical account of the parents of Eros captures this selfishness perfectly. Poverty ($\pi\varepsilon\nu\acute{\iota}\alpha$) is his mother, Contrivance ($\pi\acute{o}\rho o\varsigma$) his father. For this reason, Eros is always poor, and far from being sensitive and beautiful, Eros is hard, weather-beaten, shoeless, and homeless, taking after his mother. However, as his father's son, he schemes to get what is beautiful. Eros is bold, clever, always devising tricks to get what he wants (*Symposium* 203b–e). To the selfishness of Eros, Freud (1930, 117–113) adds the ease with which Eros is drawn into the service of aggression. Theoretically distinct, practically they often become one.

Caritas is different. A Latin dictionary will usually give the first definition of caritas as dearness or high price. *Amor* may be used of animals, whereas caritas applies only to human relations. While the Greek Eros may be rendered by the Latin amor, caritas has a richer set of connotations than the Greek *philia*. The Greek *agape* comes close, but it doesn't seem quite fair to use a term so closely associated with Christian love to characterize reparation. In turning to the term caritas, I mean to suggest that for Klein, cultivated reparation and the depressive position are a type of love that truly cares about the integrity and otherness of the other. Caritas begins in guilt, for it knows that one has wished to take all the other has to give, and throw the empty husk away. But caritas ends in reparation, which longs to make sacrifices on behalf of the other, in order to restore the wholeness one has longed to plunder.

To be sure, caritas too is subject to the risks of reparation. Even caritas requires cultivation and guidance. That's what the natural law is for.

One must be careful about ideals of lost wholeness, as Christopher Lasch (1991) and Jean Bethke Elshtain remind us.

If we pretend to a primordial wholeness that no longer exists – or try to create one through grandiose philosophies that know no limit – we fall into a form of self-idolatry; we make believe that we are pre-lapsarians, that we are once again innocents in the Garden, that we have known no evil. Self declared innocents are more likely to be drawn to optimism rather than drawn to that hope linked to recognition of our estrangement and our need for faith and fellowship. (Elshtain, 1999)

Fortunately, neither Klein nor Maritain idealize lost wholeness. Though both mourn its loss, both understand that whatever wholeness is to be regained is but a shadow of its ideal, a shadow whose darkness is created by human hatred, greed and evil, passions that can at best be kept at bay, never conquered, never transformed, never overcome. Neither Klein nor Maritain purchases her or his optimism cheaply. Indeed, for both the appropriate term is not optimism but hope, a point to which I shall return.

Maritain credits Thomas as his inspiration, but he came to Thomas and the natural law only after listening to Henri Bergson's lectures on phenomenology. Indeed, the story goes that Jacques and Raïssa had decided to kill themselves within a year if they could not find an answer to the meaning of life. They found it first in Bergson, whose lectures they attended in 1901. Presumably Bergson lectured about what he published several years later – that one could find an absolute nonrational type of knowledge through intuition, what has come to be known as connaturality.

By intuition is meant the kind of intellectual sympathy by which one places oneself within an object in order to coincide with what is unique in it and consequently inexpressible. . . . There is one reality, at least, which we all seize from within, by intuition and not by simple analysis. It is our own personality in its flowing through time – our self which endures. . . . What is relative is the symbolic knowledge by pre-existing concepts, which proceeds from the fixed to the moving, and not the intuitive knowledge which installs itself in that which is moving and adopts the very life of things. This intuition attains the absolute. (Bergson 1955, 23–24)

For Maritain, "natural law" meant not that it exists "out there" in nature, but that it exists within, and is known by a type of innate knowledge that is as indubitable as any feeling, such as "I feel sad," or "I feel happy."

Exactly how this innate knowledge operates remains unclear, but for Maritain and his followers, the practices of poetry, aesthetics and music seem to be the leading similes, though it would be more accurate to call them points of access. Listening "to the melody produced by the vibration of deep-rooted tendencies made present in the subject" when the subject is confronted with the suffering, pain, and longing of its object, is how Maritain (2001, 34–35) puts it. This is how the natural law is known. Absolutely committed to a realist epistemology, for Maritain natural law refers to how we know this world of moral feeling rather than whether it exists, or whether the external world that evokes it is real.

One can't say quite the same thing about Klein. Nevertheless, she too is committed to innate knowledge, not just of good and bad breasts, but of the far more complex innate knowledge that is love, hate, and reparation. And the experience that draws forth this innate knowledge is similar to that of Augustine. Only instead of stopping at the overwhelming individual experience of the goodness of the world, and hence the One who made it, this innate knowledge includes the overwhelming individual experience of the badness of the world that frustrates and denies me gratification, a world that I would destroy in my frustrated rage if I could. Not only that, but I would suck the good world dry, take it all in if I could, leaving nothing for others, nothing for the good world itself. I would become the good world, with nothing left over. This, as Milton's Satan reveals, *is* evil.

For most, this knowledge remains unconscious, which does not mean we do not act on it everyday of our lives, and so make it real. Not only the desire to consume the goodness of the world, coupled with the desire to destroy what I cannot consume, but the desire to make reparation to those whom I have harmed and damaged in phantasy and reality, generally remains unconscious. Unconscious knowledge does not mean dormant knowledge, however. Unconscious knowledge may be put to work through poetry, art, and literature, resonating with deep-rooted tendencies in a subject who loves his or her object, much as Maritain writes about the melody of the natural law. Indeed,

an unfolding passionate dynamic like that described by Klein pro-
duces the vibration that plucks the heartstrings that Maritain writes
about. What Maritain adds is what the Kleinian account so desperately
needs: intellectual and moral guidance to caritas, the love of reparation, so that caritas is not rendered self-indulgent, turned-inward, and
so become merely art. In this regard, at least, the Kleinian account is
primary. Natural law provides the direction; reparation the passion.
This, at least, has been my argument.

What about the darker dimension of Klein, the way in which she, like
Freud, understands that the balance between love and hate is so terribly close, that Thanatos may carry the day. Isn't Maritain a cockeyed
optimist by comparison? Yes and no. To be sure, Maritain sees history
as providential; he could see it no other way. But that is only from
the perspective of eternity. If human nature is fundamentally good,
its basic goodness is "joined to a swarming multiplication of particular
evils." The result "is the very mystery and the very motive power of the
struggle and progression in mankind" (Maritain 1942). In other words,
"the devil hangs like a vampire on the side of history. History goes on,
nonetheless, and goes on with the vampire" (Maritain 1957).[4] This
is an image of history that Klein could appreciate, the blood-sucking
Furies hanging onto the great train of history, seeking to leach the life
out of human progress. There will be no Great Reparation, not in this
world, only living with the devil.

Maritain was not a consistent thinker, and he wrote these thoughts
under the impress of World War Two, an experience which led Maritain, like so many others, such as Arendt, to struggle with the introduction of a new type of evil into the world, a new paganism Maritain called
it. Civilization, he said, had entered the "end of an age," one which
began with the fall of Rome. Nevertheless, while Maritain's thought
is providential, as it must be for a Christian thinker, it is not cheaply
optimistic.

In what does Maritain's providential thinking consist? In hope.
Not that the world will necessarily make progress and become better.
Though much of the time Maritain seemed to believe progress was

4 I have turned to Richard Crane's "Maritain's True Humanism" (2005, 19–21) in my
discussion of Maritain's view of history.

inevitable, the events of World War Two and the Holocaust seemed to have led him to doubt this, at least in the scale of human generations that we have become familiar with in measuring these things. But hope as Christopher Lasch (1991) defines hope, not that everything will work out all right in the end (the human end that is, not the eschaton), but that we shall be able to make sense of it all, because the curtain was once parted for us, and we have seen the end in the beginning, the word made flesh (John 1:1–19). The result is not just knowledge of the end. Perhaps that is not even so important. The result is knowledge of how to live in this world.

And how is that? With caritas, under the guidance of the principles of personalism, Maritain's most characteristic doctrine, though hardly his alone. Personalism regards individuals as having rights much as liberal or bourgeois individualism does, but the argument is different, as these rights stem from seeing each individual *imago Dei*. Maritain wrote for *Esprit*, the personalist journal founded in 1930 by Emmanuel Mounier (1952), who believed the collapse of capitalism was imminent. Seeking to combine the insights of Marx and Kierkegaard, personalism might equally well be conceived as the child of phenomenology and Christianity! In any case, Maritain believed that the distance between personalism and liberalism was shorter than the distance between personalism and any of the other available options, such as Marxism.

Utopian, generating a social ideal that respects the individual while remaining communalist, pluralist, and theist – these are the themes generally associated with personalism. I am tempted to say that if you can imagine what this looks like in practice, then you have a better imagination than I. Yet, such a grand leap of the imagination may not be necessary. Glendon (2001, 42, 227–228) hints that the "dignitarian" tenor of the preamble of the United Nations Declaration of Human Rights, discussed in Chapter 2, comes closer to personalism than any other doctrine. One would like to be able to say that this is due to Maritain's great influence and intellectual authority, but sadly that was not the case. The UNESCO philosophers were marginalized during the document's drafting. Whatever the influence of "personalism," it was through the cultural traditions of Asia and Latin America. In other words, the influence of personalism is more likely a convergence. My point is that it does not take an act of utopian imagination to picture the social reality of personalism. Just read the UN Declaration of Human Rights, paying particular attention to its preamble.

As with most utopias, personalism is most useful in generating social criticism. The social criticism that stems from personalism is similar to that stemming from Orwell's particularism, asking us to focus not on ideologies, but people and their particular moral situations, which include the pressure of material circumstances. Personalism does not deny material reality, claiming only that men and women are not reducible to it, either through their labor, their consumption, or their biochemistry.

Though he has nowhere identified himself as a personalist (as far as I know), the political thought of Václav Havel (1995, 49–50) is consonant with personalism, which embraces individualism and democracy, but fears for the loss of human mystery, what once was called soul.

The relativization of all moral norms, the crisis of authority, the reduction of life to the pursuit of immediate material gain without regard for its general consequences – the very things Western democracy is most criticized for – do not originate in democracy but in that which modern man has lost: his transcendental anchor, and along with it the only genuine source of his responsibility and self-respect. . . . Given its fatal incorrigibility, humanity probably will have to go through many more Rwandas and Chernobyls before it understands how unbelievably shortsighted a human being can be who has forgotten that he is not God.

Have we not moved very far from Klein by this point? Yes, and it was never my intent to demonstrate the absurd thesis that Maritain and Klein are "really" saying the same thing, for of course they are not. Yet, let us not overlook the deep correspondences. Both Maritain and Klein write of the passionate struggle between good and evil for the soul of humanity. Both know that only love, not the love of Plato and Freud (that is, not Eros), but caritas, will save us. And both know, Klein perhaps even better than Maritain, the guilt that accompanies all our acts of contrition and reparation. As guilt should, for in our heart of hearts we have wished destruction of the good. In our hearts, we have been Milton's Satan.

What Maritain knows that Klein does not is not only God, but history, the way in which this struggle between good and evil takes place not merely in individuals, but in groups, communities, and societies over time. It is this, and not "only" his belief in God, which allows Maritain to transform reparative morality into the natural law, understood as the historical experience of morality. Or as Maritain puts it, natural law "develops in proportion to the degree of moral experience and self-reflection, and of social experience also, of which man is capable in the various ages of his history" (2001, 38).

The result is that Maritain solves – or rather, is finally in a position to solve – the problem that bedevils Klein, the fundamentally self-centered nature of reparation. Caritas is not enough. Even caritas requires moral and intellectual guidance, what I have called paying attention. One way to think about the natural law is as guidance in paying attention – that is, thinking about what one is doing. Only now we see more clearly than before that this is not just an individual act, but the task of history and culture.

In emphasizing the difference between Klein and Maritain in the previous paragraph, I have in one respect moved closer to Bion. Bion's great struggle is not just with thinking, but with the problem of how to get thought out of the theater of the mind, so that it might make contact with reality, and so contribute to responsible reparation. Indeed, much of Bion's work with groups can be understood as an extension of this struggle, as he came to understand the way in which groups struggle to do anything but confront the reality of the difficult tasks that face them (Bion 1961). Nevertheless, there is a way in which Bion's focus on thought keeps him confined in the theater of the mind, at least in comparison with Maritain. So concerned is Bion with thought that the objects of thought get short shrift, even as his project is to make contact with them. If you are mightily concerned that the arrow hit the bull's eye, but spend all your time and attention on the archer's technique, none on the pattern of the arrows as they miss or strike the target, you are never going to get it right.

For Maritain, the enemy is transcendentalism, idealism, and every metaphysics that overvalues the contribution of mind to reality. One cannot put Bion in any of these camps, just as one certainly could not put Orwell there. Nevertheless, Bion's focus on thought, at the expense of the object thought about, unlike Orwell, has the result of rendering Bion's approach idealistic. Richard Wollheim (1984, 216–218) has suggested that this is characteristic of every psychoanalytic approach, and perhaps he is correct. My approach to the natural law uses the British Object Relations tradition in psychoanalysis to account for our terrible hatred and destructiveness, which in turn helps to explain our overwhelming desire to make reparation. My approach also recognizes that left to itself, reparation will never be fully moral. In other words, the powers revealed by psychoanalysis motivate morality; they are insufficient to guide it.

Maritain is fascinated with poetry precisely to the degree that poetry turns us gently away from the inner world. Poetry is the intuition of (everyday) being; poetry takes the existence of things seriously. John Hittinger has as lovely quote from Nathaniel Hawthorne about some summer squash he planted. While not technically poetry, Hawthorne's prose captures this attitude toward the world.

Gazing at them, I felt that, by my agency, something worthwhile living for had been done. A new substance was born into the world. They were real and tangible existences, which the mind could seize hold of and rejoice in.

Hittinger continues,

Hawthorne surely has the germ of Maritain's intuition of being in this appreciation of squash's 'victorious thrust over nothingness' . . . After witnessing the loss of the world in abstraction, Hawthorne attends to the lowly squash and savors the glory of its being. Maritain, I think, would be delighted to have these prophetic poets return us to the savor of being as they call forth that intuition. (Hittinger 2002, 210–211)

One could go on and on trying to make sense of Maritain's intuition of being. For me, the concept is best understood as Iris Murdoch understands the vision of the artist. "He sees the earth freshly and strangely but he is ultimately part of it, he is inside the things he sees and speaks of as well as outside them. He is of their substance, he suffers with them" (Conradi 2001, 17). Even the least creative may become artists in this sense, artists of everyday living.

Not only have we gone some distance from Klein, but also from Bion. But I never claimed to demonstrate the absurd proposition that Maritain and the British Object Relations theorists were really talking about the same thing. Obviously not, and not only because Maritain's is a deeply religious vision. Maritain's intuition of being, his longing to participate in the flow of being, is not unique to his religious perspective, but it is not central to the perspectives of Klein and Bion.

If, however, we focus less on the intuition of being, and more on Maritain's personalism, then there is an unexpected continuity with Klein, albeit one found neither in Klein herself, nor Bion, but in another of Klein's students, Winnicott. As it turns out, it is not the continuity between Klein and Maritain, but the more complex continuity and discontinuity between Maritain and the British Object Relations tradition, that is our real topic.

A contemporary of Bion, Winnicott captures much, but of course not all, that personalism aims at, particularly the ideal of the individual who is at once communal, that is deeply attached to others, while retaining a mysterious, inner core, forever silent and unknowable.[5] While I shall not focus on the intuition of being in discussing Winnicott, one could say that for Winnicott nothing is more important than the mother's intuition of the child's being, which includes a profound sense of when to participate in the child's being, and when to step back in awe, wonder, and respect. This principle Winnicott extends to friends, lovers, and even citizens. This is what "holding" means.

The ordinary devoted mother, as Winnicott calls her, is with her child so that her child can be alone. Because mother is attuned to her child and its needs, the child need not be constantly attuned to mother's moods and wants. Her child is free to be, which includes being free to imagine that he or she is omnipotent, though it might be more accurate to say free to imagine that the world is ideally suited

---

[5] Personalist philosophy analyzes the meaning and nature of individual existence. While acknowledging the mysterious character of human existence, personalism remains open to the possibility of investigating this mystery, while affirming that no theory or concept can ever fully explain human life. The human person is infinitely complex, an awesome mystery. Personalist philosophers hold that experience ought to be the starting point for the philosophical analysis of the person. In this regard they reveal the influence of phenomenology, their dominant philosophical (as opposed to theological) influence. Reflection upon experience accents the unique aspects of being human, namely, consciousness and freedom. From *www.acton.org/research/dictionary*. Key figures in the intellectual history of personalism include Emil Brunner, the young Pope John Paul II, Emmanuel Mounier, Martin Buber, Max Scheler, and Gabriel Marcel. Emmanuel Levinas wrote a number of pieces for *Esprit*, several of which are now back in print. See Alford (2002).

to his or her needs. "I am hungry, and lo milk appears." This is what the child imagines when mother is in tune.

Attunement it is called in contemporary attachment theory, the psychology of the relationship between parent and child, in which a type of emotional mirroring takes place, as the child is comforted when the parent reflects and modulates the child's mood and feeling, often in another modality. For example, mother coos when baby smiles. Attunement is how humans are comforted, their emotional extremes contained, as mother calmly rocks a crying baby. Attunement is how holding is practiced. Attunement is comfort beyond, or beneath, words, the first comfort, the first communion.

> Stern . . . sees attunement as the basis for the emerging sense of self in the pre-verbal infant. Tracking and attuning . . . permit one human to be with another in the sense of sharing likely inner experience on an almost continuous basis. . . . This is exactly our experience of feeling-connectedness, of being in attunement with another. It feels like an unbroken line.[6]

Attunement *is* human attachment. Not just the clinging of Harry Harlow's monkeys, but the sense that another human being is in tune with what you feel, so that you know that you are not imprisoned in a hermetically sealed emotional world (Blum 2002). When you hurt, I feel sad, and you can see it in the slump of my shoulders. That's attunement, and music is a fine metaphor, the instruments in an ensemble in tune with each other, and themselves.

This will be a frequent experience if the mother is in tune with her child, frequent enough in any case so that the child need not confront his or her own terrible dependence for awhile. The result is the birth of creativity, in which the infant believes in his capacity to create a reality that corresponds to his or her needs. As Winnicott puts it, the baby says (wordlessly of course), "I just feel like . . . milk, a breast, a nipple," and just then the mother comes along and offers the baby her breast.

> We have to say that the baby created the breast, but could not have done so had not the mother come along with the breast just at that moment. The communication to the baby is 'Come at the world creatively, create the world;

---

[6] Jeremy Holmes (1993, 156), quoting Daniel Stern, *The Interpersonal World of the Infant* (1985).

it is only what you create that has meaning for you.' Next comes 'the world is in your control.' From the initial *experience of omnipotence* the baby is able to experience frustration and even to arrive one day at the other extreme from omnipotence, having a sense of being a mere speck in the universe...Is it not from *being God* that human beings arrive at the humility proper to human individuality? (Winnicott 1987, 100–101, his emphasis)

While his model is mother and baby, Winnicott makes much the same point about friendship. It too is based upon the capacity to be alone while in the presence of another. In friendship, the attunement is mutual, but the principle is the same, each friend responsive to the other while taking care not to intrude upon each other's sacred space, which Winnicott imagines as residing in an untouchable part of the self, unknowable even to the subject, but evident in such moments as the spontaneous gesture (Winnicott, 1965b, 33).

The problem between friends, even between citizens (though it takes a political community, once known as a polis, to make this a problem in the first place), is to stay related without being penetrated, to remain connected without being compromised. Just being left alone won't help, not even under liberal individualism and market capitalism. To be left alone is to have to care for oneself constantly, which means never being free to just be. Perhaps the enthusiasts of civil society have found that place to be, though one wonders how much satisfaction there can be in bowling with others when one is scared stiff about losing one's job. (*Bowling Alone* by Robert Putnam [2001] is not only the single most well known work on the decline of civil society; it has become metaphor for the decline.)

Winnicott is not the psychoanalyst of personalism, but he is a psychoanalyst for whom the contradictory elements of personalism are at home. To be sure, there is hardly a speck of religious awe to be found anywhere in Winnicott's work. But there is awe aplenty, if by awe we mean respect for the mystery and wonder of what it means to be an individual, a self, a person. How do persons come to be, why are individuals so fragile, how is it that so many people appear to be selves but upon closer examination seem to be play acting? These are the questions Winnicott asks, understanding that his answer will never be adequate to the question. Finally, Winnicott understands the great irony of individualism: that it takes a community for individualism to come into being. Like the good enough mother, like the good friend, this community must stand back far enough from the individual to let the individual be, without dropping or abandoning the individual in his or her hour of need. If the community can do this, then the individual can come to acknowledge his or her terrible dependence on others without abandoning his or her fragile self. The scale is different, but the logic is the same as that of the good enough mother and the child who would be God, but in the end only to know his or her smallness.

Brief Didactic Summary

I have introduced several concepts: thinking as linking, containment or holding, of which personalism is the social-theoretical dimension, reparation, and caritas, not to mention the natural law. What is the relationship among these concepts? Allow me to be didactic for a moment, even if it is not quite so simple as my summary.

The experience of being held or contained, being neither dropped nor crushed, an experience expressed in personalism (but not only in that doctrine) is necessary in order for thinking as linking to occur; otherwise, we defend ourselves against dread by shattering the links between thoughts and feelings. Doing so is tantamount to shattering the links between thoughts themselves, every thought a little feeling.

Thinking as linking, so similar to what Orwell calls paying attention, is unnecessary for the emergence of the strong desire to make reparation; reparation is nature's passion. But nature's passion is irresponsible, self-indulgent, in need of direction and guidance.

Caritas is a natural expression of the love that lies behind reparation. Yet, even about caritas we should not be sanguine. Because we desire what is best for others does not mean that our love will be able to provide it (to believe that one's love is enough would itself be mock reparation). One of the bitterest fruits of adulthood is the knowledge that our care cannot shield those we love from anguish, despair and death. The culture too will make an enormous difference in its members' ability to care well for each other. Consider, for example, a culture which defines parental care as preparing one's child for life in a winner-take-all economy. Unless one pays thoughtful attention, caring for one's child will mean teaching him or her not to care for others.

What are we to conclude? John Hittinger, following Maritain, concludes that "the political task, therefore, is 'essentially the task of civilization and culture'" (Hittinger, 2002, 12). I would conclude the same, with this emendation. The political task in question is realizing the natural law, and one does so by creating a civilization and culture of containment. Only in such a culture can its members feel free enough, secure enough, to transform caritas into a principle of everyday living. I will elaborate on this conclusion shortly, after first considering how not to think about the natural law.

THE IMPLICATION IS NOT EVOLUTIONARY
NATURAL LAW

Natural law is not just what we naturally want to do, including making reparation. Natural law is about what we should do, what we ought to do. How best to think about the obligation inherent in natural law – what is the way in which natural law has traditionally bound nature and moral obligation? This is my concern for the remainder of this chapter. Indeed, it should be the leading concern of anyone who takes seriously the natural law.

First, however, I must make explicit an argument regarding how *not* to think about this natural obligation. We should not think about it in the language of the evolutionary natural law, probably the single most influential narrative under which the natural law is discussed today. Evolutionary natural law has a peculiar link to Klein, via its frequent reliance upon John Bowlby's attachment theory. While in training to become a psychoanalyst, Bowlby was analyzed by Klein, as well as by a leading student of Klein's, Joan Riviere. One might be tempted, therefore, to think that evolutionary natural law could be a step in the direction I am taking. Nothing could be further from the truth.

Elaine Scarry (1985) writes that torture unmakes the world, making it impossible for us to put ourselves back together again. Winnicott makes much the same point about a much more subtle phenomenon, the failure of attunement and attachment, what he calls holding, especially in early life, but throughout the life cycle. The result is not so much an inability to put ourselves together again, but that we have to do all the work ourselves, with the result that we can never just relax and be.[7] The relevance to natural law is this. Most of us will do anything to belong to the group. Most of us will do anything not to be emotionally abandoned, not to be left out in the cold. Humans are creatures of attachment, creatures of belonging. It is not for nothing that Antigone is a hero of the natural law (even if her story is more complex): she goes against human nature in the name of a higher nature. It is not for nothing that the aspect of psychoanalytic thought that has been drawn upon most frequently to support the natural law runs from Winnicott's theories of holding and attunement, through John Bowlby's (1969) attachment theory to Larry Arnhart's (1998) *Darwinian Natural Right: The Biological Ethics of Human Nature*, an account of natural law from the perspective of evolutionary theory. Indeed, MacIntyre (1999, 12, 125) finds much to admire in Arnhart's evolutionary account of Saint Thomas, and natural law generally, particularly the way in which evolutionary theory appreciates human dependence, the theme of MacIntyre's recent book.

The reasons I find this line unconvincing are several. First, because I believe that Klein deals with even deeper matters, the struggle of love and hate for the life of the human species. The second is that Hume and the naturalistic fallacy, while not posing an insuperable obstacle to empirical explanations of natural law, nonetheless need to be addressed, not ignored. The third reason is the simplest and most important. If human beings are creatures of attachment and belonging, as likely to do their evil out of a fear of not belonging as out of a love of destruction (as Augustine insists), then a natural law morality based strictly upon the virtues of belonging will at best be only half the story. The terrors of abandonment and exile may come closer to the love of destruction than we know; indeed, they may feed off each other.

Nevertheless, one can see the appeal of a natural law morality based upon the appeals of belonging: evolutionary ethics, as it is called. Throughout the Western world, and nowhere more than the United States, individualism is rampant, or perhaps I should just call it selfishness, what Tocqueville calls egoism (*égoïsme*). Some argue that greed

---

[7] To anyone who has suffered torture, I apologize; certainly I recognize the vast difference between torture and emotional abandonment, arguing only that there is a continuum for certain purposes.

is good; too much social and political theory idealizes individual freedom and choice as the highest values. How gratifying it is to learn
that greed and selfishness are not any more natural than cooperation,
self-sacrifice, and altruism. The trouble is, most of the truly horrible
acts in history have been committed not by selfish individuals, but by
ordinary men and women following orders. We must consider whether
evolutionary ethics adequately addresses this problem. Can evolutionary ethics discover the sources of resistance to malevolent authority?

Consider Stanley Milgram's (1974) famous studies of *Obedience to
Authority*. Milgram too refers to evolutionary ethics to account for the
high levels of obedience he uncovered. Unlike Arnhart and other
evolutionary ethicists, Milgram is not comforted by group selection.
On the contrary, Milgram (writing during the Cold War) warns that
group selection may kill us. Not malevolence, but obedience to duly
constituted authority, seemed most likely to lead to World War Three.

For the sake of argument, let us assume that everything Peter
Corning (2003) says about evolutionary ethics is true.

1. Evolutionary ethics refers to a phenomenon that is material,
   something real in the natural world.
2. Evolution works not just through individual selection, but group
   selection.
3. One reason group selection is not readily seen is that the distinction between altruistic and egoistic behavior is drawn too
   sharply; much socially responsible behavior is both, as I benefit
   from belonging to an effective group.

If this is so (and I believe that it is), then should we all just agree and
go home early? Not just yet, for the possibility exists that evolutionary
ethics may, in some circumstances, be immoral. More precisely put, in
some circumstances evolutionary ethics is not helpful in distinguishing
moral from immoral behavior.

Recall Milgram's famous experiments in obedience to authority.
Originally, he tells us, he had planned to conduct his experiments in
postwar Germany, investigating the sources of German obedience to
authority. As it turned out, Milgram never left New Haven, finding
levels of obedience to authority there he never imagined.

The experimental situation was devilishly simple. A naïve subject,
called the "teacher," is ordered to give what he believes are powerful,

potentially fatal, electrical shocks to a mild-mannered middle-aged man who says he has a heart condition. Coming onto the experimental stage (for that is what it was), the subject faces a shock generator with levers running from 15 to 450 volts in 15-volt increments. The levers are labeled, from "mild shock" to "dangerous shock," "extremely dangerous shock," and "XXX." Each time the "learner," actually a confederate of Milgram, fails to remember a word pair, he ostensibly receives a shock. The shocks increase in 15-volt increments. For the first mistake, the learner receives a 15-volt shock, for the next mistake a 30-volt shock, and so on. The experiment is designed so that the learner makes a lot of mistakes, requiring that he receive numerous shocks of ever increasing intensity.

Under the voice-proximity condition, as it is called, the "learner" begins to grunt with discomfort at about 100 volts. As the shocks grow stronger, he yells, screams, complains of his heart condition, demands to be released (he is strapped into his chair, electrodes clamped to his arm), and finally falls silent.

How many subjects would deliver the full battery of shocks? Milgram asked a panel of psychiatrists, and they estimated one-tenth of one percent, the sickest and most sadistic members of the population, potential Brown Shirts. In fact, almost 65% of the subjects, working- and middle-class men living in New Haven, delivered the full battery of shocks under the voice-proximity condition. To be sure, the teachers did not ignore the learner's cries. Many hesitated, a number demurred, but when ordered to continue delivering the shocks, most did.

Struggling to explain the high levels of obedience he discovered, Milgram turns to evolutionary ethics as the most likely explanation, arguing much as Corning does that natural selection has favored those groups of humans whose members readily defer to legitimate authority. Humans are born to obey. Obedience stabilizes the group, minimizing conflict within the group, allowing the group to be more effective in conflict with other groups. In response, it might be argued that Milgram is writing about the problem of obedience to malevolent authority, whereas evolutionary ethics is concerned with the origins of social cooperation. In fact, these are not separate phenomena; obedience to legitimate authority is a big part of what it means to cooperate socially.

Milgram, like Augustine, takes great pains to argue that his subjects are not sadistic; they find no joy in harming others. Indeed, anyone who has seen the films of the experiment would be hard put to argue that they do. Nevertheless, Milgram has no special access to their motivation, and one can imagine that what subjects want, what subjects desire, what subjects have found is the heavenly city for normal sadists – that is, sadists with a guilty conscience, a little like you and me. Here the average man or woman (women were as obedient as men) was given the chance to inflict hurt and pain on a weak, vulnerable, and innocent man, but all in the name of science, and all under conditions under which they can deny their pleasure, because they can deny their choice.

"I didn't do it because I wanted to; I did it because I was ordered to, because I didn't have any choice." For some this seems to be the perfect combination, the double pleasure of hurting without having to take responsibility for it. This, at least, would explain what Milgram otherwise found so puzzling, eventually passing it off as a bizarre reaction to the tension of being placed in a morally and psychologically impossible situation. Almost forty percent of his subjects, depending upon the experimental conditions, reacted with embarrassed smiling, grinning, and laughter.

Might they also have laughed out of the guilty, shameful pleasure of it all? Perhaps not just the pleasure of delivering what the subjects believed were powerful electrical shocks to an older middle-aged man with a heart condition, but the pleasure of becoming one with the experimenter, the source of all power and authority within the laboratory that had become the world. Recall that Augustine believes it was his bonding with the other young men that led him to steal and despoil the pears. Yet, Augustine remained troubled, as well he should. Perhaps the greatest pleasure of all is the guilty pleasure of shared domination and destruction, a pleasure all the greater because it is forbidden. This Augustine intuited, even if he never quite knew what to do with this knowledge.

Consider for a moment a more recent study, Christopher Browning's (1992) account of a group of *Ordinary Men*, a group of older reservists from Hamburg who were ordered during the fading days of National Socialism to shoot Jews. Their commander, Major Trapp, was hardly enthusiastic. On the contrary, he stated publicly that anyone who could not stomach such an order (which included shooting women and children at close range) could stand aside. They would face no repercussions. Hardly any of the men took Trapp up on his offer (at first fewer than five percent; eventually less than twenty percent). In seeking to explain the hesitancy of these less than eager murderers to stand aside, Browning cites peer pressure (as we call it today) as the main reason. These ordinary men could not bear the informal censure of their fellows. They could not bear being considered slackers, ones who failed to do their duty: not to Hitler, or even to Trapp, but to their fellow soldiers.

The problem with the Nazi's, says Eli Sagan (1988, 11–13), is not that they had too little superego, but too much. Superego isn't that little voice that tells you right from wrong. It is that little voice that tells you to follow the commands of legitimate authority, which includes the informal expectations of one's peers. There is, in other words, not that much difference between obedience and conformity within the group. In many circumstances, the group is the legitimate authority, as it was for Browning's ordinary men.

You see, of course, where all this is heading. Whether being an engaged, dutiful, respectful, caring member of the group is good depends on whether what the group is doing is good. Evolutionary ethics explains the bases of social cooperation. It does not, and cannot, tell us whether this cooperation is good. That depends on what the group is doing – that is, on whether the group is good.

Almost in passing, Corning mentions that one of the good things to come out of the terrorist attacks on the United States of 9/11 was the sense that for a little while Americans were all in this together, that many were not just willing but eager to sacrifice for others, such as donating blood and money. More than a few sacrificed their lives. Trouble is, evolutionary ethics, understood as the built-in tendency of humans to cooperate, and even sacrifice, in the name of the group, explains the behavior of the terrorists as well as their victims. Like their victims, the terrorists gave of themselves to the group, caring more about a shared ideal than their own lives. Corning does not discuss the power of shared ideals; yet it is this, as much as the more mammalian forms of attachment about which he writes, that binds human groups together. Human attachment is mediated by symbols, not just skin and kin.

What makes the ethics of the terrorists wrong? About this question evolutionary ethics is not very helpful. Evolutionary ethics is concerned with the relationship between me and my group as it faces other groups in the competition for scarce resources, which for human animals includes meaning. In the case of the terrorists, the scarce resource is the meaning of modernity itself. Evolutionary ethics helps to explain as a point of empirical fact why individuals sacrifice for their group. In doing so it tells us about a force that no one concerned with social or ethical theory can ignore. What evolutionary ethics cannot do is tell us what we should do. In other words, evolutionary ethics is an empirical account of the bonds that hold a group together. It cannot tell us which groups and societies should be held together, which shouldn't, and why.

Consider the following simple example from Arnhart. "The Catholic Church's prohibition of divorce is contrary to the natural pattern of human mating" (1998, 265). True enough, but is this bad or good? Darwinian natural right tells us that banning divorce will put pressure on human nature. Many will fail the test. But, as Aristotle's *Nicomachean Ethics* (1109a1–35) tells us, the most valued human excellences are precisely those that are the most difficult to achieve. Knowing that the Church forbids a practice that is contrary to the natural pattern of human mating tells us that the Church is asking something difficult of us. But we knew this already, and have known it collectively for over two thousand years (Mt 19:1–12). What we don't know is whether the Church should ask this, and about that question evolutionary ethics has hardly a word to say.

One might read my comments as simply the application of the naturalistic fallacy to evolutionary ethics: you can't derive ought from is. In fact, it's not so simple. Evolutionary ethics speaks to a deep need among many social and political theorists, including myself, to find the natural basis of what they already know: how deeply humans are bound to each other, how much they care about each other, indeed how much they often (not always!) want to sacrifice for others. Such behavior is not only moral; it is inspiring.

Trouble is, the people we want to sacrifice for (when we do) are the members of our own group. No matter how large, no matter how symbolically mediated (for example, all who pledge allegiance to the American flag), our group is not coextensive with humanity. To imagine that it is the social function of religion to extend evolutionary ethics to all humankind misunderstands evolutionary ethics, to say nothing of turning religion into an adjunct of global sociology. Evolutionary ethics assumes the group, in competition with other groups, is the fundamental unit of analysis, the entity for which men and women live and die. This is true whether the group is my country, my corporation, my ethnic group, perhaps even my extended family. Generally, it is actual lives that are being sacrificed; sometimes it is mere livelihoods, as when academic departments battle over scarce university resources, a particularly wretched instance of group selection, but for this reason no less real.

While evolutionary ethics binds nature to moral obligation, the moral obligation it is concerned with is insufficiently general: "my group," which no matter how large and encompassing it may be, is by definition not coextensive with humanity. It can't be; for "my group" in competition with other groups is the entity with and upon which group selection works.

It is in this context that questions such as when one should refuse to sacrifice for one's group, and on what basis, arise. And it is in this context that evolutionary ethics is unhelpful. Or rather, evolutionary ethics is helpful in precisely the empirical sense to which Arnhart refers (or should be referring) when he says that banning divorce goes against human nature. So does standing up to one's group. This is why people should sometimes do it. This is why Antigone remains an inspiration. But exactly when should we stand up to our group? Evolutionary ethics offers hardly a clue.

The natural law of reparation, in conjunction with thinking about what one is doing, offers quite a few clues, particularly in conjunction with the personalism of Maritain and Winnicott. To be sure, reparation + thinking about what one is doing + a focus on the particular = no definitive answer. But this equation sets the individual against the group while defining the individual in terms of his or her relationship to the group. This is the proper place to be in order to think about these issues, a place that is at once connected to the group and yet separate from it. There is no other decent place to be as far as ethics is concerned.

BINDING NATURE AND OBLIGATION

Natural law is not just what we naturally want to do, including making reparation. Natural law is about what we should do, what we ought to do. If we are to reject evolutionary ethics, then how best to think about the obligation inherent in natural law – that is, the way in which natural law has traditionally bound nature and moral obligation? Consider the following everyday example.

Imagine that Peter is the most important person in the world for Joan. You know this because she has told you this many times over lunch. Suddenly Peter dies, and Joan just goes on with her life, hardly pausing to go the funeral. You would have to say (unless you think Joan was lying) that Joan does not yet really know that Peter has died, and that it will take a while for the knowledge to sink in. When it does she will be devastated. Certain types of knowledge, it appears, are inseparable from our emotional response. Or rather, our emotional response *is* knowledge (Nussbaum 1990, 41).

One may say much the same thing about thinking about what one is doing. Truly thinking about what one is doing, thinking as linking, means that one feels not just the need to make reparation, not just the desire to make reparation, but the obligation to do so. One is obligated because the conjunction of thinking about what one is doing and reparation means that one cannot understand one's envy, hatred, and sadism (that is, the presence of the death instinct behind so much of what one does) without feeling an overwhelming responsibility to make reparation. Experienced fully only in the depressive position, in which one knows how much one has hated as well as loved, reparation feels obligatory, the only conceivable response to such grave and dreadful passions directed not just at the world in general, but toward those we love and care for.

That such grave and dreadful passions are merely human, all too human, may make them less grave and dreadful when we stand back from ourselves, seeing these same passions in friends and others whom we know to be basically good souls. Experiencing these emotions in oneself, a version of thinking as linking, offers no such consolation, only the obligation of reparation. In a word, the experience of reparation is inseparable from the obligation to act. The problem is that even when we have overcome our tendency to project our hate into others, and so experience reparation in terms of the moral obligation to act, this obligation may be turned inward and become art. This has its place, but a decent culture will constantly draw us back into the real world, even as it uses the artistic impulse to do so. Reparative natural law quite rightly contains the word ought, as in "You ought to make reparation to those you have harmed in reality, and to those most deserving; you should not just retire to your room, study, or studio in order to let your inner world repair itself. In other words, you ought to mend others, not just yourself. As a member of society, you are involved in the ruin of humankind."

Aren't you committing the "naturalistic fallacy" a thoughtful reader might reply? No. Sentences such as "you ought to make reparation to those you have harmed and to those most deserving" do not stand alone. They are what it means to experience the reparative impulse, an expression of human nature, while thinking about it in a culture of containment.

Aristotle said it is the task of the lawgiver to make good men by habituating them to good works (*N. Ethics*, 1103b3–5). What might this mean in light of our considerations? That it is the task of the political leader to make the links, habituating citizens to thinking. It is the task of the lawgiver, in other words, to put thoughts together for those who can't. Needless to say, few political leaders are able to do this; even fewer are willing to try. The task requires courage and psychological attunement in equal measure. Especially important is sensitivity to what citizens can bear to know, and what must remain unsaid and unknowable, at least for now. To some degree this skill can be taught, but it is in good measure intuitive, even unconscious. That is all to the good. Politicians who sound like psychologists will not find many listeners, at least not for long.

If one is looking for an example of a politician able to link unthinkable thoughts, Václav Havel (1992) provides a good example. This short passage from his celebrated New Year's Address of 1990, the first of his presidency of Czechoslovakia, demonstrates both Havel's ability to link what has so long been held separate, as well as his capacity to provide a context of understanding which says in effect that knowledge previously held in separate watertight compartments need not destroy us when the doors are opened and the waters rush in.

The worst thing is that we live in a contaminated moral environment. We fell mortally ill because we became used to saying something different from what we thought. We learned not to believe in anything. We have to accept this legacy as a sin we committed against ourselves. If we accept it as such, we will understand that it is up to us all, and up to us only, to do something about it. We cannot blame the previous rulers for everything.

It is no exaggeration to say that Havel's speech, so bound to his exemplary life, provided political therapy for a citizenry mired in decades of evil.

By evil I mean politically inspired attacks on linking: the demand that citizens not know (or at least act as though they didn't know, which over a period of time can amount to almost the same thing) what they experienced every day of their lives. And if the Velvet Revolution was in the end disappointing, one need only compare it to the disintegration and hell that overcame Yugoslavia to appreciate the real, practical difference between carefully crafting links versus exploiting the death drive in order to destroy the links between being, hating, knowing, and doing.

All this talk about leadership and obligation is very nice, the critical reader may reply, but it doesn't begin to overcome the naturalistic fallacy. The felt obligation of reparation is just that, a felt obligation, not an implication of the natural law. True enough, but sentences such as "you ought to make reparation to those you have harmed and to those most deserving" do not stand alone. They are what it means to experience the reparative impulse, an expression of human nature, while thinking about it in a decent culture, one that provides social containment and moral direction to one's reparative impulses. Aquinas (ST I–II, 94, 4, 6) and Maritain both understand this about natural law: that it develops not just, or even primarily, in the individual, but in society and culture over time in which the individual participates. "For the knowledge of the primordial aspects of natural law was first expressed in social patterns rather than in personal judgments" (Maritain 2001, 35).

Facts are discovered in nature; values are created by the human decision to observe them. This is the distinction the naturalistic fallacy asks us to remember. Though the designation "metaphysical" is sometimes employed to characterize the naturalistic fallacy, G. E. Moore (1993) seems quite right that it is really a "definist fallacy" (not his term), in which the problem is that an ethical claim must eventually rest on the claim that something in the world, such as reparation, or pleasure, is good. But that is itself the question, in the end solved by definition, as Moore argues.

"Avoid the naturalistic fallacy" is a piece of practical advice for clear thinking in some circumstances. What is real is that from the day of our birth we experience the world in terms of the values of good and bad: good is what soothes and satisfies, bad is what frustrates and agitates. It is the task of a decent culture to make sure that this original experience of natural value corresponds to our highest values. A decent culture fosters the ability to think about what one is doing, and so directs the reparative impulse toward those most deserving. Within a decent culture it makes perfect sense to say that the obligation to make reparation is a fact, not just a value. Or rather, there is no meaningful distinction to be made. Alasdair MacIntyre (2000) and John Searle (1969, 175–198) have made this argument at length, so there is no need to pursue it further here.

Like inclination, reparation is not so much an instance of the natural law as how we know it. This is why thinking about what one is doing is so central to an account of natural law under the cultivated passion of reparation – that is, pity. As long, that is, as one understands thinking as a type of thinking-feeling, which comes close to what Maritain means by inclination, listening to "the melody produced by the vibration of deep-rooted tendencies made present in the subject" (Maritain 2001, 34–35).

But melodies generally require, if not an orchestra, then at least an ensemble.[8] My inner melody must resonate with the world: not necessarily the larger world, which may have become corrupt, but with more than me. Otherwise expressed, words do not exist in a vacuum; they are always part of an institutional context. Consider the following passage from the philosopher R. M. Hare, quoted by John Searle (1969, 190). "If a person says that anything is red, he is *committed* to the view that anything which was like it in the relevant respects would likewise be red."[9] Among these "relevant respects" presumably is the wavelength of the light reflected by the object. Consider what the term "committed" means in this sense. Or rather, consider what gives the

---

[8] An ensemble refers here to a small group of soloists who perform together. I chose my musical analogy carefully, keeping in mind Socrates' famous claim that it would be better for me "that my lyre or chorus I directed should be out of tune and that multitudes of men should disagree with me than that I, being one, should be out of harmony with myself, and contradict me" (*Gorgias* 482c). My view of natural law as narrative is not in agreement with Socrates, but with the Socratic dialectic.

[9] I follow Searle's (1969) argument closely in this paragraph and the next. The emphasis on the term "commitment" in the quote by Hare (1963, 11) is Searle's.

statement about the red object the force of a commitment. Not the terms themselves, but the institutional context, such as the agreement among English speaking scientists to call "red" the color of any object that reflects light of a certain wavelength. (Ordinary English speakers come to a similar, if less formal, agreement about what to call "red.")

How is this agreement different from the agreement among the citizens of a decent culture to call harming innocents a bad act that commits the harmful one to making reparation? Certainly one could not claim that the statement "the object is red" possesses an objective status in the way that the claim "harming innocents is bad" does not. Both conclusions are the result of thousands of years of cultural, historical, and scientific development. Why, then, do so many persist in seeing a fundamental difference between these two conclusions? Because they assume that there exist independently identifiable classes of descriptive and evaluative statements. This is true, however, only in specially constructed languages, not the language of life, which includes the language of Aquinas, Maritain, and Klein, as well as that of Aristotle.

"Aristotle takes it as a starting-point for ethical enquiry that the relationship of 'man' to 'living well' is analogous to that of 'harpist' to 'playing the harp well.'" Within this framework one can "derive" ought from is, just as one can derive the statement "a good watch ought to keep the correct time" (*N Ethics*, 1095a 16; MacIntyre 1981, 56–57). To call an action right is to say what a good man would do in such a situation; hence the statement is factual. Within this way of thinking – that is, within an ethical tradition – moral and evaluative statements can be called true or false. Within a decent culture, the obligation to make reparation is as much fact as value.

This is what Anthony Lisska (1998) means when he says that Aquinas's natural law ethics avoids the naturalistic fallacy because the developmental aspects of human nature already implant an ought within the is. We experience the world as a world of oughts from the beginning of life. Properly cultivated, the result is not the derivation of ought from is, but the education of this primordially ought-driven experience of the world so that it becomes more refined, more moral. I am making precisely the same argument about an account of the natural law of reparation.

In fact, this is essentially Hume's position, a point that is sometimes overlooked. Hume objects to the attempt to derive oughts from statements of empirical fact (*Enquiry Concerning the Principles of Morals,* Appendix 1). Hume does not object to attempts to derive oughts from statements about feeling. On the contrary, Hume believes that certain moral feelings, such as the revulsion against vicious tyrannies, possess the status of moral certainties. It is to this example that he refers when he states that "the general opinion of mankind has some authority in all cases; but in this [case] of morals it is perfectly infallible. Nor is it less infallible because men cannot distinctly explain the principles on which it is founded" (*Enquiry Concerning the Principles of Morals,* III, 2, 9) Indeed, it is statements like this that led Frederick Copleston (1959, vol. 5, 34) in his *History of Philosophy* to portray Hume as a virtual natural law theorist. But that's not quite right either. Hume is a moral sense theorist, holding that our "'oughts' can indeed be reliably engendered by internal sentiments, common to the majority of humankind, registering our reactions to the states of affairs that reason recognizes as existing" (Kainz 2004, 73).[10]

Isn't that all I'm claiming for Klein? No, or if it is, then the moral sentiments are constantly at war with the immoral sentiments, including hate, greed, and the desire to spoil the moral sentiments simply because they are moral. There is no room for (indeed, no conception of) *this* conflict in Hume. This is a conflict that can only be acted out on a world historical stage, and it is one that must be contained there too, if it is not to destroy the species. In other words, the conflict of moral and immoral sentiments (to use Hume's language) can and must draw every human institution into the struggle, lest it torment the individual unto death, destroying civilization in the process. It is only by wrapping these dueling moral sentiments in that double connective tissue of caritas and culture that it becomes more accurate to speak of these sentiments as natural laws. Moral sentiments institutionalized in a culture of containment are natural laws.

It would be easy to read my argument as saying that reparation is the content of the true natural law. That's true, but it is more important to see why: because human destructiveness and malevolence, indeed the love of destruction, is far greater than any of the natural law theorists, including Augustine, who came closest, ever imagined. Not Augustine,

---

[10] Kainz (2004, 70–73) was helpful on the relationship between Hume, moral sentiments, and the natural law.

but Milton's Satan, grasped the true extent of human evil, only it is a property not just of Satan, but of us all.

The difference with Satan is that most of us are, at some level, appalled at our own love of destruction, particularly when we recognize that we hate those we love and care for. The task of the natural law is to direct our fear, our guilt, our love, and above all our desire to make reparation, toward those who most truly deserve our love, including their most deserving stand-ins. Matthew 25: 34–45 provides a few hints as to who these might be. Left untutored, reparation is likely to give up too quickly, turning inward, or going off in a half-dozen morally irrelevant directions.

The terrible twentieth century has contributed much to this insight, so that the goodness that Augustine writes of, to say nothing of the evil that is allegedly the mere absence of goodness, is no longer a compelling account of history. I have tried to convey the way in which the reparative natural law may take this historical world seriously, but only when we understand reparation, linked to thought, as a response to the hatred that each of us is capable of, as well as the cultivation of hatred which groups regularly practice.

Reparative natural law exists neither in a vacuum, nor in some abstract realm akin to Plato's forms. Reparative natural law exists in each one of us, but it exists more precariously than Aquinas, or even Augustine, ever grasped, more deeply and permanently threatened by the death drive than any of the natural law theorists ever imagined. That this death drive may become a permanent part of the culture, so that it comes to be seen as a normal way of life, is the risk we face today (not a historically new risk, but a trenchant one): that we may become the new German robbers (ST I–II, 94, 4, 6), immune to the promptings of natural law, all too susceptible to natural hate.

CONCLUSION

Does any of the empirical research in Chapter 2 support reparative natural law? Not at first glance. To be sure, I could get people to talk reparative talk. That was the idea behind question 7 (see appendix to Chapter 2). But of all the questions, 7 generated the emptiest and most pro-forma responses. Not, I believe, because it was about reparation, but because it had the double misfortune of being excessively hypothetical (in effect it asks the informant to imagine being twenty-five years older), while clearly having a right answer.

While nothing about the social contract in either of the forms in which it was expressed by about eighty percent of informants (metaphysical biologists or self-evident social contract theorists) was reparative, for both groups the social contract represented a container, a fleshy human web, albeit one with surprisingly large holes. A sense of feeling contained is, I have argued, a necessary condition for responsible reparation, a necessary condition of thinking as linking, under which reparation may become moral. Indeed, for a number of metaphysical biologists, who in one way or another justified Articles 1 and 3 of the UN Declaration of Human Rights in terms of "we all come from the same place," the social contract had the quality of a collective birthplace, albeit not a terribly comforting one, meeting only nominal standards, a barely adequate hospital in a third-world country.

Informants were neither utilitarians, nor Kantian universalists. Nor did I find more than a single example of the much feared (or admired) relativist. Informants talked about human ethical relationships as rooted in primordial human connections in a way that is little represented among academics who write about these things. Though most informants used the *language* of social contract theory, they talked about the social contract in a way that came closer to the traditional natural law, in so far as the contract was seen as based not on agreement but in the nature of minimal obligations inherent in shared human relationships and human nature. This isn't reparation, it isn't even the beginning of reparation, but it is a way of thinking about human relations compatible with reparation, more compatible than many more familiar academic alternatives.

Informants are not intellectually sophisticated, but neither are they fools; for the most part they are reasonably thoughtful men and women. An approach that begins where they begin is itself within the tradition of the natural law. Within this tradition, it is frequently held that natural law represents judgments we have already made, and could not help making, given the fact that we are human beings on this planet (McInerny 2000, 1). We may however, not yet know what these judgments are, and our culture (low culture and high culture alike) is working overtime at distracting us from finding out. If so, then it makes sense to begin with some basic moral judgments (so basic that they alone are insufficient to define a decent culture) that men and women say they have made and go from there. The fact that it is a long road from where these men and women are to where they could be is good reason to be serious and sad (depressed in the Kleinian sense of the term) about where informants in particular, and our culture in general, have ended up. It is no reason to reject informants' views out of hand, or mischaracterize their views as something they are not, such as relativism, or even liberalism.

Liberalism and the truncated natural law are the opening lines (or plot outlines, if the reader prefers that I not mix my literary metaphors) for two quite different stories. Let us not confuse them any more than they already are. Let us take advantage of what there is to work with in the culture, more I think than most of us imagine, more than some culture critics would evidently care to know. As I argued in Chapter 2, metaphysical biology, while hardly an image of man or woman *imago Dei*, provides an abstract (because it is based on an idea) but body based and hence real, not ideal, sense of commonality (but not community) among all persons.[11] What we have in common comes first. Here is the nonliberal, nonindividualistic basis of the minimum natural law. The implication is not elevated, but it has little to do with the liberalism, relativism, or most of the other "isms" that many critics of the culture seem to find there.

How might cultural workers take advantage of this insight? They might begin by talking with each other, their readers, and their students about why someone violates the (metaphysical) social contract when physically harming another, but not by lying to him or her. They might do this even if they think they know the answer, for here is a case where going over old ground, in this case putting words to feelings, is not a waste of time. The limits of care in mass, indeed, global, society is another topic open to fruitful discussion. If we recognize the natural right of every man, woman, and child to live in a state of physical security, doesn't this imply the right to live in economic security as well? And what about the right to emotional security, what I have called a

---

[11] As in Chapter 2, I include "the social contract as a basic good in itself" as a version of metaphysical biology, even as metaphysical sociology might be a more accurate term.

sense of social containment? As a practical, empirical matter, are any of these rights realizable when those who possess them feel they are about to fall out of this world?

This is what we ought to talk about today, trying to overcome another sense of what Nietzsche calls nihilism, in which the highest values devalue themselves, so that everything and everyone is equal, life the only common denominator (*Gay Science*, sections 346, 347). So minimal is the truncated natural law to begin with, almost every informant is at risk of succumbing to this sense of nihilism. Many have.

Talking and teaching aimed at filling out the content of the minimal natural law is best undertaken not by long lectures about the natural law, and certainly not by deriving this or that favorite conclusion, but by telling and discussing stories, as Richard Rorty has argued. For Rorty, the goal is to see "them" as "one of us," and this is "a task not for theory but for genres such as ethnography, the journalist's report, the comic book, the docudrama, and especially the novel" (Rorty 1989, xvi). It wouldn't hurt to include the greatest western founding document of them all, the Bible. But, even with this addition, I would still put it differently from Rorty. The goal is not simply the inclusion of the other, but the cultivation of richer inner worlds, so that people come to see the natural law not as some minimal measure of humanity, but a way of talking about the community that we all share, a community that begins with vulnerable bodies and selves, but includes so much more.

The reader would draw absolutely the wrong lesson from my work if he or she concluded that only a series of long-term, depth-psychological interviews could determine if reparative natural law exists. Reparative natural law is first of all natural law. In the tradition, natural law is located neither deep inside the individual, nor far outside, somewhere in the cosmos. (One might argue that Aquinas would locate Eternal Law there, but for Aquinas, Eternal Law is everywhere [ST I–II, 93, 2–3].) Natural law is found first in the relationship of the individual to the community. Looking for the reparative natural law deep inside the individual would be looking in the wrong place, confusing the sources of reparation with the natural law, which is the conjunction of reparation, thinking about what one is doing (thinking as linking), and cultural development as cultural containment. A continuation of the investigation begun here seems the only way to follow the ironic path by which we continue to search for what we already know, the natural law.

If the way people think about the social contract comes close (albeit in paradoxical and disappointing ways, as the content is so minimal) to the traditional natural law, then let us look at how societies, communities, and political leaders have used this minimal container, this fleshy web with gaping holes, to practice the reparative natural law, as well as to make a mockery of it, via attacks on linking. Seen from this perspective, reparative natural law is distinguished as much or more by its absence as its presence. This does not, by the way, make my claim about the reparative natural law nonfalsifiable (Popper 2002). It would be absurd to claim that both the presence and the absence of reparative natural law are equal evidence of its existence.

Broken links and shattered connections take work. The more awful the act, the more work is required. Not just (or even primarily) to destroy one's knowledge of the act, but to destroy one's knowledge about what the act means, how it is connected to everything else I know, and most of all how I would have to change and grow if I acknowledged the act (Bion 1984, 98–99). Arendt's *Eichmann in Jerusalem* is a case study of this awesome destructive effort. So is Sophocles' study of Creon in *Antigone*. The death drive is so powerful, particularly when it is organized into groups and led by charismatic leaders (and it doesn't take much charisma; the attraction of being allowed to act out the death drive contains most of the appeal), that often the clearest expression of reparative natural law is the incessant destructive work necessary to keep feelings and thoughts that might otherwise culminate in pity from coming together. When thought remains broken to pieces, unconnected to itself, and so unable to know what it is thinking or doing, when pity becomes strictly self-pity, this itself is evidence of how much work is being done to keep reparation from coming into being.

One might see my argument coming closer to Reinhold Niebuhr than either Augustine or Aquinas. Reparation, nature's gift of grace, takes both good fortune, above all the emergence of reparative leaders such as Václav Havel at a time when citizens will have them, as well as the long hard work of civilization, in order to bring reparation under the horizon of thought. Rarely is history so blessed. Let us not forget, however, that we as individuals do not require history's blessing in order to follow the reparative natural law; nor do the communities we live in, if we are privileged enough to do so. Consider too the families in which, if we are fortunate, we learn about love from our spouses, while raising our children, helping to raise our grandchildren, all perhaps while caring for our aging parents. Here is an ideal place to learn, practice, remember, and teach the reparative natural law. I conclude with families not because families don't come first. In many ways they do, but because families are a model for the natural law, not its locus. The locus of the reparative natural law is everywhere one human pities another.

References

References to classical sources are cited in the form that is usual in classical studies. This includes Augustine's *Confessions*, as well as his *City of God* and *On the Trinity*. References to Aquinas's *Summa Theologica*, abbreviated in the text as ST, are also given in the text in the form that is usual in classical studies. The same applies to references to Aquinas' *Summa Contra Gentiles*. John Milton's *Paradise Lost* is cited in a similar fashion, and abbreviated PL in the text. I follow the usual practice of citing Nietzsche's *Gay Science* by section number.

Adorno, Theodor. 1983. *Prisms*, translated by Shierry Weber Nicholsen and Samuel Weber. Cambridge, MA: MIT Press. [reprint edition]

Alford, C. Fred. 1989. *Melanie Klein and Critical Social Theory*. New Haven, CT: Yale University Press.

Alford, C. Fred. 1990. "Melanie Klein and the *Oresteia* Complex." *Cultural Critique* 15 (Spring 1990): 167–190.

Alford, C. Fred. 1997. *What Evil Means to Us*. Ithaca, NY: Cornell University Press.

Alford, C. Fred. 2002. *Levinas, the Frankfurt School, and Psychoanalysis*. Middletown, CT and London: Wesleyan University Press and Continuum Books.

Alford, C. Fred. 2005. *Rethinking Freedom: Why Freedom Has Lost Its Meaning and What Can Be Done to Save It*. New York: Palgrave Macmillan.

Arendt, Hannah. 1965. *Eichmann in Jerusalem: A Report on the Banality of Evil*, revised and enlarged edition. New York: Viking Press.

Arendt, Hannah. 1973. *The Origins of Totalitarianism*, new edition with added prefaces. New York: Harvest Books.

Arendt, Hannah. 1978. *The Life of the Mind*. New York: Harcourt Brace. [one volume edition]

Arendt, Hannah. 1996 [1929]. *Love and Saint Augustine*. Edited by Joanna V. Scott and Judith C. Stark. Chicago: University of Chicago Press.

Arnhart, Larry. 1998. *Darwinian Natural Right: The Biological Ethics of Human Nature*. Albany: State University of New York Press.

Bellah, Robert et al. 1985. *Habits of the Heart: Individualism and Commitment in American Life*. Berkeley: University of California Press.

Bergson, Henri. 1955. *An Introduction to Metaphysics*, Translated by T. E. Hulme. 2nd revised edition. Indianapolis: Bobbs-Merrill.

Bion, Wilfred R. 1961. *Experiences in Groups*. New York: Basic Books.

Bion, Wilfred R. 1984. *Second Thoughts: Selected Papers on Psycho-Analysis*. New York: Jason Aronson.

Bion, Wilfred R. 1989. *Learning From Experience*. London: Karnac.

Bloch, Ernst. 1986. *Natural Law and Human Dignity*. Translated by Dennis Schmidt. Cambridge, MA: MIT Press. ["Translator's Introduction," vii–xxx]

Bloom, Alan. 1988. *Closing of the American Mind*. New York: Touchstone Books.

Blum, Deborah. 2002. *Love at Goon Park: Harry Harlow and the Science of Affection*. Cambridge, MA: Perseus Books.

Bobbio, Norberto. 1993. *Thomas Hobbes and the Natural Law Tradition*. Translated by Daniela Gobetti. Chicago: University of Chicago Press.

Bourke, Vernon. 1988. "Natural Law, Thomism – and Professor Nielsen," in *Saint Thomas Aquinas on Politics and Ethics* edited by Paul Sigmund, 217–221. New York: W. W. Norton.

Bowlby, John. 1969. *Attachment*, New York: Basic Books.

Browning, Christopher. 1992. *Ordinary Men: Reserve Police Battalion 101 and the Final Solution in Poland*. New York: Harper-Collins.

Butler, Judith. 2000. *Antigone's Claim: Kinship between Life and Death*. New York: Columbia University Press.

Camus, Albert. 1972. *The Plague*. Translated by Stuart Gilbert. New York: Vintage Books.

Chasseguet-Smirgel, Janine. 1994. "Brief Reflections on the Disappearance in Nazi Racial Theory of the Capacity to Create Symbols," in *The Spectrum of Psychoanalysis*, edited by A. K. Richard and A. Richards, 233–241. Madison, CT: International Universities Press.

Chaucer, Geoffrey. 1993. *The Canterbury Tales: A Complete Translation into Modern English*. Translated by Robert Ecker and Eugene Crook. Palatka, FL: Hodge and Braddock, Publishers.

Clarke, Simon. 2004. "The Concept of Envy: Primitive Drives, Social Encounters, and *Ressentiment*." *Psychoanalysis, Culture and Society* 9 (1): 105–117.

Conradi, Peter. 2001. *The Saint and the Artist: A Study of the Fiction of Iris Murdoch*. New York: Harper Collins.

Copleston, Frederick. 1959. *History of Philosophy*, volume 5. Westminster, MD: Newman Press.

Corning, Peter. 2003. "Evolutionary Ethics," *Journal of Politics and the Life Sciences* 22 (1): 50–58.

Crane, Richard Francis. 2005. "Maritain's True Humanism," *First Things* (150): 17–23.

Devine, Philip. 2000. *Natural Law Ethics*. Westport, CT: Greenwood Press.

Dougherty, Jude P. 2003. *Jacques Maritain: An Intellectual Profile*. Washington, DC: Catholic University of America Press.

Edmundson, Mark. 2004. "The Risk of Reading: Why Books Are Meant to Be Dangerous," *The New York Times* August 1, 2004, pp. 11–12 (magazine section).

Elshtain, Jean Bethke. 1995. *Augustine and the Limits of Politics*. Notre Dame IN: University of Notre Dame Press.

Elshtain, Jean Bethke. 1996. "The Mothers of the Disappeared: An Encounter with Antigone's Daughters," in *Finding a New Feminism*, edited by Pamela Grande Jensen, 129–148. Landover, MD: Roman and Littlefield.

Elshtain, Jean Bethke. 1999. "Limits and Hope: Christopher Lasch and Political Theory," *Social Research* (Summer) (66): 531–543.

Euben, Peter J. 1990. *The Tragedy of Political Theory*. Princeton, NJ: Princeton University Press.

Evans, G. R. 1982. *Augustine on Evil*. Cambridge: Cambridge University Press.

Feyerabend, Paul. 1993. *Against Method*, 3rd edition. London: Verso.

Finnis, John. 1980. *Natural Law and Natural Rights*. Oxford: Clarendon Press.

Freud, Sigmund. 1899. "Screen Memories." *The Standard Edition of the Complete Psychological Works of Sigmund Freud*, edited and translated by James Strachey et al. London: Hogarth Press, 1953–1974, vol. 3, 303–332. [Hereafter cited as *The Standard Edition*.]

Freud, Sigmund. 1915. "Thoughts for the Times on War and Death," [Appendix: Letter to Dr. Frederik Van Eeden] in *The Standard Edition*, vol. 18, 275–302.

Freud, Sigmund. 1920. "Beyond the Pleasure Principle," in *The Standard Edition*, vol. 18, 3–66.

Freud, Sigmund. 1930. "Civilization and its Discontents," in *The Standard Edition*, vol. 21, 59–148.

George, Robert P. 1992. "Natural Law and Human Nature," in *Natural Law Theory: Contemporary Essays*, edited by Robert P. George, 31–41. Oxford: Clarendon Press.

George, Robert P. 1999. *In Defense of Natural Law*. Oxford: Clarendon Press.

Gewirth, Alan. 1978. *Reason and Morality*. Chicago: University of Chicago Press.

Gilligan, Carol. 1982. *In a Different Voice: Psychological Theory and Women's Development*. Cambridge, MA: Harvard University Press.

Glendon, Mary Ann. 2001. *A World Made New: Eleanor Roosevelt and the Universal Declaration of Human Rights*. New York: Random House.

Greenberg, Irving. 1977. "Cloud of Smoke, Pillar of Fire: Judaism, Christianity, and Modernity after the Holocaust," in *Auschwitz: Beginning of a New Era?*, edited by E. Fleischner. New York: KTAV Publishing House.

Griffiths, Paul J. 2004. "Orwell for Christians," *First Things* (December) (148): 32–40.

Grisez, Germain 1965. "The First Principle of Practical Reason. A Commentary on *Summa Theologiae* 1–2, Question 94, Article 2," *Natural Law Forum* 10: 168–201.

Grotius, Hugo. 1964. *On the Law of War and Peace*. New York: Wiley and Sons. [Original *De Jure Belli ac Pacis*, 1625.]

Hall, Pamela. 1994. *Narrative and the Natural Law: An Interpretation of Thomistic Ethics*. Notre Dame, IN: University of Notre Dame Press.

Hardy, Barbara. 1968. "Towards a Poetics of Fiction: An Approach through Narrative," *Novel: A Forum on Fiction*, vol. 2, no. 1: 5–14.

Hare, R. M. 1963. *Freedom and Reason*. Oxford: Clarendon Press of Oxford University Press.

Hart, H. L. A. 1994. *The Concept of Law*, 2nd edition. Oxford: Clarendon Press of Oxford University Press.

Havel, Václav. 1992. "New Year's Address," in *Open Letters: Selected Writings, 1965–1990*, edited by Peter Wilson, 390–396. New York: Vintage Books.

Havel, Václav. 1995. "Forgetting That We Are Not God," *First Things* (March) (51): 47–50.

Hegel, Georg Wilhelm. 1920 [1835]. *The Philosophy of Fine Art*, translated by F. P. B. Osmaston. London.

Hinshelwood, R. D. 1989. *A Dictionary of Kleinian Thought*. London: Free Association Books.

Hittinger, John. 2002. *Liberty, Wisdom, and Grace: Thomism and Democratic Political Theory*. Lanham, MD: Lexington Books.

Hittinger, Russell. 2003. *The First Grace: Rediscovering the Natural Law in the Post-Christian World*. Wilmington, DE: ISI Books.

Hochhuth, Rolf. 2002. *Die Berliner Antigone*. Reinbek bei Hamburg: Rowalt.

Holmes, Jeremy. 1993. *John Bowlby and Attachment Theory*. London and New York: Routledge.

Kainz, Howard. 2004. *Natural Law: An Introduction and Re-examination*. Chicago: Open Court.

Kant, Immanuel. 1960. *Religion within the Limits of Reason Alone*. Translated by Theodore Greene and John Silber. New York: Perennial.

Kant, Immanuel. 1991. *The Metaphysics of Morals*. Translated by Mary Gregor. Cambridge: Cambridge University Press.

Kierkegaard, Søren. 1957. *The Concept of Dread*. Translated by Walter Lowrie. Princeton, NJ: Princeton University Press.

Klein, Melanie. 1964. "Love, Guilt and Reparation," in *Love, Hate and Reparation*, edited by Klein and Joan Riviere, 57–119. New York: W. W. Norton.

Klein, Melanie. 1975a. "Early Stages of the Oedipus Conflict," in *Love, Guilt and Reparation and Other Works 1921–1945*, 186–198. New York: The Free Press. [Volume 1 of *The Writings of Melanie Klein*.]

Klein, Melanie. 1975b. *Narrative of a Child Analysis*. New York: The Free Press. [Volume 4 of *The Writings of Melanie Klein*.]

Klein, Melanie. 1975c. "Envy and Gratitude," in *Envy and Gratitude and Other Works 1946–1963*, 176–235. New York: The Free Press. [Volume 3 of *The Writings of Melanie Klein*.]

Klein, Melanie. 1975d. "Mourning and its Relation to Manic-Depressive States," in *Love, Guilt and Reparation and Other Works 1921–1945*, 344–369. New York: The Free Press. [Volume 1 of *The Writings of Melanie Klein*.]

Klein, Melanie. 1975e. "Infantile Anxiety-Situations Reflected in a Work of Art and in the Creative Impulse," in *Love, Guilt and Reparation and Other Works 1921–1945*, 210–218. New York: The Free Press. [Volume 1 of *The Writings of Melanie Klein.*]

Klein, Melanie. 1975f. "The Importance of Symbol-Formation in the Development of the Ego," in *Love, Guilt and Reparation and Other Works 1921–1945*, 219–232. New York: The Free Press. [Volume 1 of *The Writings of Melanie Klein.*]

Klein, Melanie. 1975g. "Some Reflections on 'The Oresteia,'" in *Envy and Gratitude and Other Works 1946–1963*, 275–299. New York: The Free Press. [Volume 3 of *The Writings of Melanie Klein.*]

Kristeva, Julia. 2001. *Melanie Klein.* Translated by Ross Guberman. New York: Columbia University Press.

Kuhn, Thomas. 1996. *The Structure of Scientific Revolutions*, 3rd edition. Chicago: University of Chicago Press.

Lasch, Christopher. 1979. *The Culture of Narcissism.* New York: Warner Books.

Lasch, Christopher. 1991. *The True and Only Heaven: Progress and Its Critics.* New York: W. W. Norton.

Likierman, Meira. 2001. *Melanie Klein: Her Work in Context.* London: Continuum.

Lisska, Anthony. 1998. *Aquinas's Theory of Natural Law: An Analytical Reconstruction.* Oxford: Oxford University Press.

Lyotard, Jean-François. 1984. *The Postmodern Condition: A Report on Knowledge.* Translated by Geoff Bennington and Brian Massumi. Minneapolis: University of Minnesota Press.

MacIntyre, Alasdair. 1981. *After Virtue.* Notre Dame, IN: University of Notre Dame Press.

MacIntyre, Alasdair. 1999. *Dependent Rational Animals: Why Human Beings Need the Virtues.* Chicago: Open Court Publishing.

MacIntyre, Alasdair. 2000. "Theories of Natural Law in the Culture of Advanced Modernity," in *Common Truths: New Perspectives on Natural Law*, edited by Edward McLean, 99–115. Wilmington, DE: ISI Books.

Marcuse, Herbert. 1966. *Eros and Civilization: A Philosophical Inquiry into Freud.* Boston: Beacon Press.

Marcuse, Herbert. 1970. *Five Lectures: Psychoanalysis, Politics, and Utopia.* Translated by Jeremy Shapiro and Shierry Weber. Boston: Beacon Press.

Marcuse, Herbert. 1978. *The Aesthetic Dimension: Toward a Critique of Marxist Aesthetics.* Boston: Beacon Press.

Maritain, Jacques. 1942. "The End of Machiavellianism," in *The Range of Reason*, Jacques Maritain Center, Notre Dame University, www.nd.edu/Departments/Maritain/etext/range11.htm#p148.

Maritain, Jacques. 1953. *Creative Intuition in Art and Poetry.* New York: Pantheon.

Maritain, Jacques. 1957. *On the Philosophy of History.* Jacques Maritain Center, Notre Dame University, www.nd.edu/Departments/Maritain/etext/philhist.htm.

Maritain, Jacques. 2001. *Natural Law: Reflections on Theory and Practice*, edited by William Sweet. South Bend, IN: St. Augustine's Press.

McGinn, Colin. 1999. "Reasons and Unreasons," *The New Republic* 24 (May): 34–38. [Review of Scanlon, *What We Owe Each Other.*]

McGowan, John. 1998. *Hannah Arendt: An Introduction*. Minneapolis: University of Minnesota Press.

McInerney, Ralph. 2000. "Are There Moral Truths That Everyone Knows?" in *Common Truths: New Perspectives on Natural Law*, edited by Edward McLean, 1–18. Wilmington, DE: ISI Books.

Meltzer, Donald. 1978. *The Kleinian Development*. Perthshire, Scotland: Clunie Press. [3 parts in 1 volume]

Milgram, Stanley. 1974. *Obedience to Authority*. New York: Harper and Row.

Miller, Alice. 1983. *For Your Own Good: Hidden Cruelty in Child-Rearing and the Roots of Violence*. New York: Farrar, Straus, Giroux.

Miller, James. 1999–2000. "Is Bad Writing Necessary? George Orwell, Theodor Adorno, and the Politics of Language," *Lingua Franca* (December/January) (9) 33–44.

Moore, G. E. 1993 [1903]. *Principia Ethica*. Cambridge, England: Cambridge University Press.

Mounier, Emmanuel. 1952. *Personalism*. Notre Dame, IN: University of Notre Dame Press.

Murdoch, Iris. 1970. *The Sovereignty of Good*. London: Routledge.

Murdoch, Iris. 1998. "Metaphysics and Ethics," in *Existentialists and Mystics: Writings on Philosophy and Literature*, edited by Peter Conradi, 59–75. New York: Penguin Books.

Niebuhr, Reinhold. 1988. "Christian Faith and Natural Law," in *Saint Thomas Aquinas on Politics and Ethics*, edited by Paul Sigmund, 222–225. New York: W. W. Norton.

Nielsen, Kai. 1988. "An Examination of the Thomistic Theory of Natural Law," in *Saint Thomas Aquinas on Politics and Ethics*, edited by Paul Sigmund, 211–216. New York: W. W. Norton.

Nietzsche, Friedrich. 1974. *The Gay Science*. Translated by Walter Kaufmann. New York: Vintage Books.

Nussbaum, Martha. 1990. *Love's Knowledge: Essays on Philosophy and Literature*. Oxford: Oxford University Press.

Orwell, George. 1949. *Nineteen Eighty-Four*. New York: Signet.

Orwell, George. 1953 [1946]. "Why I Write," 309–316, in *A Collection of Essays*. New York: Harcourt.

Orwell, George. 1970a [1946]. "Politics and the English Language," 156–170 in *A Collection of Essays*. New York: Harcourt.

Orwell, George. 1970b [1946]. "Why I Write," 309–316, in *A Collection of Essays*. New York: Harcourt.

Pagels, Elaine. 1995. *The Origin of Satan*. New York: Random House.

Popper, Karl. 2002. *The Logic of Scientific Discovery*, 15th edition. New York: Routledge.

Prince, Gerald. 1987. *Dictionary of Narratology*. Lincoln: University of Nebraska Press.

Putnam, Robert. 2001. *Bowling Alone: The Collapse and Revival of American Community*. New York: Simon and Schuster.

Rawls, John. 1999. *A Theory of Justice*, revised edition. Cambridge: Belknap Press of Harvard University Press.

Rieff, Philip. 1961. *Freud: The Mind of the Moralist*. New York: Harper & Row.

Rilke, Rainer Maria. 2000. *Duino Elegies: A Bilingual Edition*. Translated by Edward Snow. New York: North Point Press.

Rorty, Richard. 1979. *Philosophy and the Mirror of Nature*. Princeton, NJ: Princeton University Press.

Rorty, Richard. 1989. *Contingency, Irony, and Solidarity*. Cambridge: Cambridge University Press.

Rosenfeld, Herbert. 1988. "A Clinical Approach to the Psychoanalytic Theory of the Life and Death Instincts: An Investigation into the Aggressive Aspects of Narcissism," in *Melanie Klein Today*, vol. 1, edited by Elizabeth Bott Spillius, 239–255. London: Routledge.

Rousseau, Jean-Jacques. 1964. "Discourse on the Origin and Foundations of Inequality among Men" [Second Discourse], in *The First and Second Discourses*, translated by Roger Masters and Judith Masters, 77–228. New York: St. Martin's Press.

Rudnytsky, Peter. 1994. "Freud and Augustine," in *Freud and Forbidden Knowledge*, edited by Peter Rudnytsky and Ellen Handler Spitz, 128–152. New York: New York University Press.

Rustin, Michael. 1982. "A Socialist Consideration of Kleinian Psychoanalysis," *New Left Review* 131: 71–96.

Rustin, Michael. 1991. *The Good Society and the Inner World: Psychoanalysis, Politics and Culture*. London: Verso.

Sagan, Eli. 1988. *Freud, Women, and Morality: The Psychology of Good and Evil*. Englewood, NJ: Fish Drum Press.

Sartre, Jean-Paul. 1956. *Being and Nothingness*. Translated by Hazel Barnes. New York: Washington Square Press.

Sartre, Jean-Paul. 1964. *Nausea*. Translated by Lloyd Alexander. New York: New Directions.

Sartre, Jean-Paul. 1999. "The Humanism of Existentialism," in *John-Paul Sartre: Essays in Existentialism*, edited by Wade Baskin, 31–62. Seacacus, NJ: Carol Publishing Group.

Scanlon, T. M. 1998. *What We Owe Each Other*. Cambridge, MA: The Belknap Press of Harvard University Press.

Scarry, Elaine. 1985. *The Body in Pain: The Making and the Unmaking of the World*. New York: Oxford University Press.

Schneck, Stephen. 2004. "Strauss *contra* Aquinas: The Problem of Nature for Right." Paper Presented at the Annual Meeting of the American Political Science Association, Chicago, IL.

Schweitzer, Albert. 1965. *The Teaching of Reverence for Life.* Translated by Richard Winston and Clara Winston. New York: Holt, Rinehart, and Winston.

Scott, Joanna V. and Stark, Judith C. 1996. "Rediscovering Hannah Arendt," in Hannah Arendt, *Love and Saint Augustine*, edited by Joanna Scott and Judith Stark, 115–215. Chicago: University of Chicago Press. [interpretive essay by editors]

Searle, John. 1969. *Speech Acts: An Essay in the Philosophy of Language.* Cambridge: Cambridge University Press.

Segal, Hanna. 1955. "A Psycho-Analytical Approach to Aesthetics," in *New Directions in Psycho-Analysis*, edited by Melanie Klein, Paula Heimann, and R. E. Money-Kyrle. London: Maresfield Library.

Stanford, W. B. 1983. *Greek Tragedy and the Emotions.* London: Routledge and Kegan Paul.

Steiner, George. 1986. *Antigones.* Oxford: The Clarendon Press.

Steiner, John. 1993. "Review: Narcissistic Object Relations and Pathological Organizations of the Personality," in *Psychic Retreats*, 40–53. London: Routledge.

Stern, Daniel. 1985. *The Interpersonal World of the Infant.* New York: Basic Books.

Steuerman, Emilia. 2000. *The Bounds of Reason: Habermas, Lyotard and Melanie Klein on Rationality.* London and New York: Routledge.

Strauss, Leo. 1999. *Natural Right and History.* Chicago: University of Chicago Press.

Tocqueville, Alexis de. 2000. *Democracy in America.* Edited and translated by Harvey Mansfield and Delba Winthrop. Chicago: University of Chicago Press.

Veatch, Henry. 2005 [1978]. "Natural Law: Dead or Alive?" http://oll.libertyfund.org/Texts/LiteratureOfLiberty0352/BibliographicEssays/VeatchNaturalLaw.html.

Vernant, Jean-Pierre and Vidal-Naquet, Pierre. 1988. *Myth and Tragedy in Ancient Greece.* Translated by Janet Lloyd. New York: Zone. [each author takes responsibility for particular chapters]

Weber, Max. 1958. *The Protestant Ethic and the Spirit of Capitalism.* Translated by Talcott Parsons. New York: Charles Scribner's Sons.

Winkler, John and Zeitlin, Froma. 1990. "Introduction," to *Nothing to Do with Dionysos? Athenian Drama in Its Social Context*, edited by John Winkler and Froma Zeitlin, 3–11. Princeton, NJ: Princeton University Press.

Winnicott, D. W. 1965a. "The Theory of the Parent-Infant Relationship," in *The Maturational Processes and the Facilitating Environment*, 37–55. Madison, CT: International Universities Press.

Winnicott, D. W. 1965b. "The Capacity to Be Alone," in *The Maturational Processes and the Facilitating Environment*, 29–36. Madison, CT: International Universities Press.

Winnicott, D. W. 1971. "The Location of Cultural Experience" in *Playing and Reality*, 95–103. London and New York: Routledge.

Winnicott, D. W. 1978. "Hate in the Counter Transference," in *Through Paedi-atrics to Psycho-Analysis*, 194–203. London: Hogarth Press.

Winnicott, D. W. 1987. "Communication between Infant and Mother, and Mother and Infant, Compared and Contrasted." In *Babies and Their Mothers*, edited by C. Winnicott, R. Shepherd, and M. Davis, 89–103. London: Free Association Books.

Wollheim, Richard. 1984. *The Thread of Life*. Cambridge, MA: Harvard University Press.

Young-Bruehl, Elisabeth. 1982. *Hannah Arendt: For Love of the World*. New Haven, CT: Yale University Press.

Index